Six Ha'pennies

Ian Braybrook

Marilyn Bennet Publishing
100 Brown Street
Castlemaine
Victoria 3450

This edition, 2019
First published, 2007

Copyright © Ian Braybrook 2007, 2019

All rights reserved. Without limiting the rights under copyright, no part of this publication may be reproduced, stored or introduced into a retrieval system, or transmitted in any form or by any means (electronic, mechanical, photocopying, recording or otherwise) without the prior written permission of the writer and the publisher.

ISBN 978-0-9944370-4-4

 A catalogue record for this book is available from the National Library of Australia

Cover images by Chris Rae.

Every effort has been made to locate copyright owners. We apologise for any omissions. This will be corrected on notification in future editions.

Dedicated to Andrew Arthur Braybrook, my father,
born White Horse Range, Ballarat 1892,
died Trentham 1945.

Contents

Author's note	9
Prelude	13
Chapter One	15

February 12th 1834. Inworth. The Ship. A robbery. Arrests. The trial. Death sentence. Abraham Braybrook's mother.

Chapter Two 26

Reprieve. Portsmouth. The hulks, The work. Conditions. Teachings. Meals. Shoemaking. New South Wales? A shilling a week. Give thanks to God!

Chapter Three 31

Hard work. A taste of the lash. The diet. The Britannia horror. Letters to home. Medical exams. A sea voyage.

Chapter Four 37

Port Jackson and Sydney Town, 1834. The Hooghly. *The marketplace. The people. The convicts. The women.*

Chapter Five 43

Governor Bourke. The arrival. The sea voyage. Inworth Village, Essex. Harsh U.K. laws. Unemployment. Chartists-Unions. Tolpuddle martyrs. A brush with the law.

Chapter Six 49

Henry Boucher Bowerman. 'Marion'. Parramatta. Murder, bloody murder! Lerida Creek. William Allen. 23 servants. Bombala – The High Country. Assembly at Yass.

Chapter Seven 63

Abraham's overland journey to Australia Felix begins. Leaving Yass. Yaldwyn, Brown and Allen.

Chapter Eight 66

The Murrumbidgee River. Tarcutta to Billabong Creek. Seven Mile Creek. Hot weather. Dead men's bones. Cannibals? The Murray River. Rest days.

Chapter Nine 74

The Ovens River. The Broken River. The Goulburn River. John Coppock. The Coliban River. Alexander Mollison. Charles Ebden. Forest Creek. Expedition Pass. Castlemaine. A valley of the finest description.

Chapter Ten 81
Establishing Maiden Hills Station. Jobs allocated. Bowerman comes to visit. Ten pounds a year rent for 50,000 acres. Three lonely shepherds in two tents. Eight Aboriginals slaughtered. Reprisals feared.

Chapter Eleven 91
Settling into a new camp. Shepherd's rations. Solitude. Sheep and shoes. First encounter with natives. Haircuts and meat. Female company? Allen warns natives off.

Chapter Twelve 98
Melbourne, 1839. Captain William Lonsdale. George Augustus Robinson, Protector of Aborigines. Charles Sievwright. The ride to Maiden Hills. Sievwright meets Allen.

Chapter Thirteen 111
Sievwright at the camp. The killings site. Depositions from all involved. Arrests and murder charges. Sievwright is sceptical of Allen. Off to Melbourne.

Chapter Fourteen 117
The long walk to Melbourne. The Stockade. LaTrobe and Lonsdale informed. The hierarchy alarmed. The public prosecutor intervenes. The trial and the jurymen. Charges altered. Overseer Allen appears. Controversy. A town divided. The verdict.

Chapter Fifteen 128
Learmonth brothers. Bowerman dies. Loss of the Brittania. Robinson visits Maiden Hills. Surprise meeting with Abraham. The Learmonths castigated by government. The Plenty River.

Chapter Sixteen 136
A Ticket of Leave. A Conditional Pardon. A marriage. The River Plenty. Black Thursday.

Chapter Seventeen 147
Eliza moves on. Robert Black. A marriage. Ballarat. Belfast or Belfast?

Appendix 151

Acknowledgements 155

Bibliography and References 157

Index of Names and Places 159

Other Titles by Ian Braybrook 162

Author's note

AUSTRALIA is now almost free of the dark cloud of Botany Bay, and the ignominy of our first chapter is nearly forgotten, even by those who trace their ancestors to the criminal colonies.

Ours is a country settled by convicts. Often they were little more than children, with the overwhelming majority having committed petty crimes, usually driven by the need to survive.

Many fine men and women, from many walks of life, were among those who came to our shores shackled in chains. They were farmers, artists, clerks, writers, labourers, butchers, farmhands, architects, managers. They were the thinkers and they were the doers – the heavy lifters. And of course, there were the unfortunate women and girls. Their contribution to the developing nation was vital. Sadly, they were often deplorably treated; mere chattels exploited by men; suffering dreadful misuse and abuse. It is to our shame, along with the inexcusable treatment handed to the original owners of this land.

Our convict settlers were the people who truly founded this nation; not the bureaucrats, the wealthy and the self-styled aristocrats. Convicts did the hard and exhausting work, most often in appalling, spirit-breaking conditions; to the shame of those who were responsible.

Later, these poor people were joined by hardy settlers who were scarcely any better off than the convicts. These folk were free, but in name alone.

To the convicts fell the worst and dirtiest jobs, the most dangerous and difficult tasks and plain hard work. They were men and women who were unfortunate victims of a system of slavery given a cloak of respectability in the guise of penal service. But they established Australia; from their work we built a great nation

Those of us who have convict ancestors have every reason to be proud of them. They contributed far more to the firm foundations of Australia than any others. Without them it would not have happened as it did.

For purposes of continuity and cohesion I have, at times, found it necessary to use my imagination. That aside, what you read is a true indication of the life and times of the poor people of the time.

If any writings give offence, please note that I quote directly from letters, articles, notes and material of the time, and expressions that were used then may not be acceptable today.

I also acknowledge the original ownership of the lands mentioned in this story by Australia's first inhabitants, our Aborigines. I deeply regret my great-grandfather's role in relation to conduct adverse to them. To those people I say: I am sorry.

One day Australia will be a republic, casting off the last vestige of the chains connecting us to the old British Empire that, for dubious reasons, established the first settlement here.

This is the true story of an Australian pioneer, Abraham Braybrook, 1811–1851.

Ian Braybrook
Castlemaine, Victoria.
January 2019

Prelude

THE penal transportation system had existed for centuries, and with the claiming of Australia by Britain, the establishment considered it desirable to settle this place by this means, especially since the American war of independence had shut down that human dumping ground.

The system was understandable but indefensible. Transportation was simply a form of slavery devised to further the interests of the British Empire and those who controlled it. The forced labour was made more productive by the generous use of the lash and harsh, even inhuman, punishment.

The men who controlled the colony of New South Wales were far removed from the pain, the filth, the heart-rending cruelty, the suffering and the degradation of these unfortunate people.

Prominent British lawyer, statesman and writer, Earl Frederick of Birkenhead, claimed that the system worked and worked admirably.

> 'They served their term, were set free to live a useful and productive life, better than they could at home. We should feel no shame. The wisdom and justification for the system lay in the

incontrovertible fact that it worked and worked well.'

But was the cruelty and degradation necessary? Even if it was expedient to use convicts to settle the colony, was it really necessary to manipulate the laws to ensure a steady supply of these slaves? The humiliation and suffering was disgraceful and unforgivable. Tragically, the poor of Ireland were selected to suffer even more than most.

It is little wonder that so many Australians still harbour antipathy toward Britain and resentment toward authority.

> From distant climes o'er widespread seas we come,
> Though not with much applause or beat of drum.
> True patriots all, for be it understood,
> We left our country for our country's good.
>
> *An anonymous convict*

Chapter One

February 12th 1834. Inworth. The Ship. A robbery. Arrests. The trial. Death sentence. Abraham Braybrook's mother.

In 1834, Inworth was a small village of about 600 people, situated on the Blackwater River in the county of Essex, district of Maldon, England. The nearest larger town was Kelvedon, the official 'post town' for Inworth, meaning it had a post office.

Today, Inworth has been overtaken by neighbouring Tiptree with a population of about 10 000. Despite its size, the people of Tiptree voted in 1999 to retain the title of village rather than adopt 'town', as proposed by the Essex County Council. Inworth is now insignificant in comparison to Tiptree.

The land around is fertile and undulating, with rich loam soil. It is a good farming district. In 1834, however, farming was in the doldrums, experiencing hard times, probably much like other parts of rural England. The industrial revolution had sucked men, women and children into the warrens of industrial towns where they were forced to work to exhaustion. Ten per cent of the entire population of England was on Parish Relief. In Ireland it was a staggering twenty-five per cent. Boys and girls, some as young as nine, were forced to work in mines and factories and, not uncommonly, were flogged if they refused or misbehaved.

* * *

The Ship as it was, about 1910. © John Everett, used with permission.

It was cold in Inworth on the night of February 12th 1834, but it was moonlit and clear with the usual winter mist absent and the Potter Row buildings clearly visible.

At one in the morning, only one window on the street was emitting light, a feeble yellow glow that shone through the smoke-stained bar-room window of The Ship, Inworth's only pub*. As with most pubs of the time it was the village meeting place. The hotel was run by popular publican James Emson.

Inside, gathered around the huge blazing fireplace, seated on rough hand-made chairs or leaning against the mantle, were several men. At this hour they were all a little drunk, 'freshy' as the locals called it.

There was William Parkinson, the farrier, brawny but

---

*   *An Inworth / Tiptreee hotel named* The Ship *is still open for business. It is the one referred to.*

The Ship, built c. 1300. This is the pub that Abraham drank at in 1834. Photo by Alan Braybrook, 1981.

good natured, and Timothy Hellen, a farmer, who were engaged in earnest conversation. Beside them, two old men were yarning about the events around the district; next to them were two young men, saying little as they sipped the last of their pints.

The younger of the two was fair-haired, almost six feet tall, heavily built and well muscled. He was 18-year-old Henry Pye. His companion was 22-year-old Abraham Braybrook, also tall for the time, with long, ragged brown hair that hung to his broad shoulders. His bushy eyebrows framed soft, grey eyes set in a clean-shaven face that wore the ruddy complexion of an English country boy.

Both the lads were farm labourers, but neither of them

> The Jury acquitted the prisoners.
>
> James Moss, Abraham Braybrook, and Isaac Sheldrick, labourers, were indicted for assaulting John Gager, on the King's highway, and robbing him of three sovereigns. It appeared, by the prosecutor's statement, that he was drinking, in company with the three prisoners, Pye, Howard, and others, at Rawlinson's beerhouse, at Inworth, on the 25th of February. Moss and Sheldrick betted each other 2s. that he could not produce a sovereign. This had the desired effect. Gager, eager to decide the wager by the production of his golden store, ran home, and, on his return, had no sooner placed seven sovereigns upon the table, than the plot was completed. The lights were put out, the table upset, and a general scramble took place. It appeared that the prosecutor was in a state of beastly intoxication at the time. The Jury acquitted the prisoners, and the Learned Judge refused to allow the prosecutor's expenses, observing, that he would not suffer the county to be burthened with expenses arising from so disgraceful a transaction.

A newspaper report from 1833 indicating that Abraham Braybrook 'had form'.

had had any work for several weeks. Having spent the last of their money, they could do nothing but stand by the fire empty handed. James Emson was a cheerful host but not in the habit of giving credit to unemployed farm labourers; finally the two had no choice but to make their way home. They said goodnight, and stepped out into the chilly night air. They were probably a little 'freshy', given the late hour.

By two in the morning, farmer Timothy Hellen was quite drunk and he fumbled to check the contents of his canvas money bag; he always kept a good account of his spending. He was later able to tell the court that he had spent exactly fourteen pence that night and there were six halfpenny coins left in the purse.

He decided it was time to go home, and William Parkinson, the farrier, felt the same. He joined Hellen and the two set off, bracing against the cold. They walked side by side for some

All Saints Church, Inworth is still in use. Abraham was christened here.

distance, but at the crossroads, Parkinson said goodnight and went his own way. Hellen trudged on alone toward his farm. Soon after, he observed two men walking back toward the village. He said later that he took them to be Abraham Braybrook and Henry Pye.

The moon shone brightly and lit the way ahead. A half mile from Hellen's farm, the stile that he used to cross the stone fence surrounding his farm came into view. He crossed the fence and as he stepped from the stile he was startled by a noise behind him; he turned quickly to observe two men rushing at him.

The nearest man grabbed him and threw him roughly to the ground. Quietly, the second man turned him onto his belly, thrusting a hand into the frightened man's pocket from which the assailant withdrew a piece of string, which he cast aside. The first man reached into the other pocket, locating a canvas bag. He tipped its contents into his hand and six halfpennies and a key glinted in the moonlight. He returned the items to the bag and thrust it inside his shirt.

He and his companion dashed off into the night. Not a word had been uttered.

Hellen, somewhat sobered by this experience, staggered to his feet and went helter-skelter for home.

First thing the next morning, Timothy Hellen made a call on Constable Sparrow, who accompanied him to the site of the alleged crime. Scuff marks on the ground indicated that there may have been a struggle and Hellen's walking stick lay nearby.

The farmer told Sparrow of his belief that the robbers were Abraham Braybrook and Henry Pye.

Sparrow went immediately to Braybrook's home and placed him under arrest. Pye lived in the humpy next door, and his arrest followed immediately after.

Both were taken to the lock-up at Kelvedon, and next day were walked the fourteen miles to Chelmsford to await a visit by a circuit judge who regularly conducted the county assizes there.

Theft of money was a capital offence in 1834, punishable by death. The threat of facing the hangman was real.

The trial was swift and, as the two accused young men had no counsel or knowledge of the law, it was more than a little one-sided. Hellen's evidence was presented and drew a bit of quiet laughter when he stated that he was 'quite sober' at the time of the alleged robbery. Young Abraham interjected that Hellen went home drunk and beat his wife. Undoubtedly his outburst did little to endear him to the judge.

Constable Sparrow gave his supportive evidence for Hellen, and Abraham and Henry were permitted to call witnesses on their behalf.

Abraham's mother Ann* stated that her son, 'came home between eleven and twelve and went to bed; he did not get up again until seven in the morning'. There is no mention of Abraham's father being present.

William Parkinson, the farrier, stated that Hellen was quite drunk when he left The Ship. He lived next door to Braybrook and there was only a thin partition separating the homes. He claimed that he spoke to Abraham when he came in from The Ship and the young man was in bed, so he could not have robbed Hellen.

Phillip Pye, Henry's father testified that he also lived next door to Braybrook and had heard Parkinson talking to Braybrook. Joe Reed, a lodger with the Pye family said he let Henry in at 1 am and he went to bed. He did not go out again.

The judge summed up the evidence stating that the witnesses for Braybrook and Pye had contradicted each other. The jury promptly found both men guilty and the judge sentenced them to death.

---

* *Named Mary in a contemporary newspaper report. Mary was an Aunt, and may have also been in the courtroom.*

The witnesses returned home, including Abraham's poor mother. We know no more of her or any other of Abraham's family.

Timothy Hellen also went to his home, the prosperous small farm Lucas Croft, no doubt satisfied with the judge's sentence.

Abraham Braybrook obviously had no inkling of the mishaps and adventures that were ahead of him. He could not have imagined that he would achieve considerable notoriety in the not too distant future and in a far distant land.

Opposite: A report of the trial of Abraham Braybrook from The Essex Herald. *11th March 1834.*

Abraham Braybrook, 21, and *Henry Pye*, 18, labourers, were indicted for assaulting and robbing Timothy Helen, on the King's highway, at Inworth—Timothy Helen examined. I am a farmer at Kelvedon. On the 12th of Feb. I went to the Ship at Potter Roe, and continued there till early the next morning; the two prisoners were there, and left a short time before I did. I cannot say whether they were drunk or sober—I was sober—I left about two o'clock. About half a mile from the Ship the prisoners passed me, and shortly after I got over a stile into the fields. I heard a noise behind me, and looking round saw the prisoner Braybrook coming after me; he struck me and knocked me down, but said nothing; I begged for my life. Pye then came up, and took a piece of string and other articles out of my pocket. Braybrook turned me over, and then took my purse, containing 3d. and a key, out of my pocket. They then left me.—Cross-examined. Did not drink anything besides beer, at reckoning came to 14d. I was quite sober.—By the Court. Neither of the prisoners spoke when they had me down, but I am certain they are the men. I had a good opportunity of seeing them.—Jas. Emson. I keep the Ship, at Inworth. On the night in question, the prisoners left my house about one o'clock Helen left about two; he was not intoxicated.—By the Court. Helen was waiting to see me, as I was not at home till nine.—Thomas Sparrow. I went with prosecutor the next day to the spot where the robbery took place. We then found the hat and stick prosecutor had lost the night before; there was also the mark on the ground where the prosecutor lay, and the footmarks of persons who appeared to have been standing over him.—Prisoners, in defence, said Helen went home drunk that night, and beat his wife. — Parkinson, a farrier, was called for the prisoners. He swore that he saw Helen at the Ship, and that he was then "freshy"—witness added—I live next door to Braybrook, and there is only a thin partition between the rooms; I got home about three, and spoke to Braybrook, who was in bed.—By the Court. Helen left the Ship when I did, and walked part of the way up the road with us.—Mary Braybrook, the mother, swore that her son came home between eleven and twelve, and went to bed; he did not get up again till seven o'clock in the morning.—Philip Pye swore that he heard Parkinson speak to Braybrook as he was in bed at three o'clock in the morning.—Joseph Reed said he lodged with Pye, and that he let him in at one o'clock in the morning; he went to bed, and did not go out again till 7 or 8.—His Lordship summed up, and said that as the prosecutor left the Ship at two, there was nothing inconsistent in Braybrook's being in bed at three. The statement of the mother that her son was at home between eleven and twelve was contradicted by the prisoner's own witnesses, as well as those for the prosecution, who all agreed that he did not leave till one.—The Jury found them both *guilty.*—Death Recorded.

Essex. **The Jurors** for our Lord the King, upon their Oath present, That Abraham Braybrook late of the parish of Hare Laborer and Henry Pye late of the same place Laborer on the Twelfth Day of February in the Fourth Year of the Reign of our Sovereign Lord William the Fourth, by the Grace of God, of the United Kingdom of Great Britain and Ireland King, Defender of the Faith, with Force and Arms, at the Parish aforesaid, in and upon Timothy Heller _____ in the Peace of God and our said Lord the King, then and there being, feloniously did make an Assault, and the said Timothy Heller _____ in Corporal fear and danger of his Life, then and there feloniously did put, and One Key of the value of (Sixpence) _____ one (several Bag of the value of three) pence _____

and Six pieces of the (other monies of this Realm called Halfpence) of the Goods Chattels and Monies of the said Timothy Heller _____ from the Person and against the will of the said Timothy Heller _____ then and there violently and feloniously did steal, take, and carry away, against the Peace of our said Lord the King, his Crown and Dignity. &c.

ROBBERY. INDICTMENT. 1834. ESSEX ASSIZES. REF 35/274.(1944)

The indictment against Abraham Braybrook and Timothy Pye for the assault and robbery.

(Puts himself Jury say Guilty to be hanged by the neck until he be dead. - - - - - Rep^d Trans: Life)

Essex The Jurors for our Lord the King, upon their Oath present, That Abraham Braybrook (put himself like verdict like judgment Judgment Rep^d Trans Life) late of the parish of Imworth in the County of Essex Labourer and Henry Pye late of the same place Labourers on the twelfth -- Day of Februrary in the Fourth Year of the Reign of our Sovereign Lord William the Fourth, by the Grace of God, of the United Kingdom of Great Britain and Ireland King, Defender of the Faith, with Force and Arms, at the Parish aforesaid, at the County aforesaid, in and upon Timothy Hellen - - - - - in the Peace of God and our said Lord the King, then and there being, feloniously did make and Assault, and the said Timothy Hellen - - - - - in Corporal fear and danger of his Life, then and there feloniously did put, and One Key of the value of Sixpence -- one Canvas Bag of the value of three pence - - - - - - - - - - - -
- -
and Six pieces of the Copper monies of this realm called Halfpence of the Goods and Chattels and monies of the said Timothy Hellen - - - from the Person and against the will of the said Timothy Hellen - - - then and there violently and feloniously did steal, take, and carry away, against the Peace of our said Lord the King, his Crown and Dignity.

(signed)

Indictment 1834 Essex Assizes. Ref 35/274 (1969)

A transcript of the indictment.

Chapter Two

*Reprieve. Portsmouth. The hulks, The work. Conditions.
Teachings. Meals. Shoemaking. New South Wales?
A shilling a week. Give thanks to God!*

CHAINED hand and foot, Abraham and Henry were bundled off into the cells, the judge's words ringing in their ears. They had heard that many of the death sentences were being commuted to long prison terms, but there was great uncertainty. It was not until the next morning that the Sheriff delivered the news that both Abraham and Henry had had their sentences commuted to transportation for life. They would be sent to the colony of New South Wales. In 1834 a life sentence meant for the term of a natural life. In the case of many, including Abraham, it also prohibited the prisoner ever returning to England. Despite the harshness of the sentence the men's relief is not hard to imagine. They had no real idea what their sentence actually meant. It meant all of life in the colony. 'Life' meant what it said in 1834.

The two young men, accompanied by several other unfortunates, were placed in a cart for the ten-mile journey to the port at Maldon. There was no opportunity to say goodbye to loved ones. At Maldon they were loaded onto a small coastal ship, already crammed with other prisoners, for a three hundred kilometre trip to Portsmouth. None had ever been on a ship before, and they had no idea where they were going, or how long they'd be at sea. Most thought they were being sent directly to New South Wales, and the thought of travelling to the other side of the world on the creaking old ship was terrifying. They probably believed it was the ship that would take them to wherever it was they were being sent. None among them had a clue where New South Wales was, except that some said it was in a place called Australia, at the bottom of the world.

Three days later, Portsmouth hove into view, the ship dropped anchor in Langstone Harbour, where the prisoners were ordered ashore. Their relief was short-lived as they were herded toward an enervated, rotting hulk tied up nearby. The faded name *Leviathan*, still visible on her bow, indicated that the ship had likely enjoyed a much better past. These days she was the home for 600 prisoners of the crown.

The icy cold of February whipped through the old ship's rigging and she rocked gently with the swell of the sea. The group, still chained hand and foot, were marched on board by a company of well-armed soldiers. Here they were ordered to strip naked, shivering in the cold. They were each issued their 'uniform' of dull grey, ordered to dress, and moved below deck to their quarters, known by all as The Knackers.

Their quarters were disgusting, even to those accustomed to living in squalor. Each dark and smelly cage-like cubicle measured just three metres by three metres and housed twenty men. This allowed each prisoner just under half a square metre of space for sleeping. There were no beds and each man had two rough blankets and a straw mattress, items that had been fouled by countless men before them. The stench was dreadful. The toilet was a foul bucket, which was also used for the laundry.

Abraham and his companions were soon ordered above deck where they were instructed by a senior guard on their roles and duties. They were to join work parties ashore each day, carrying out tasks on government projects and loading and unloading ships. Their work hours would be from 7 am until sunset each day excepting the Sabbath, set aside for worship of God. Given their orders, the men were then addressed by the Chaplain. He impressed on them the need to fall upon their knees and express their thanks to God for sparing their unworthy lives!

In the evenings, a number of the men were taught skills that would be useful in the colonies. Abraham was instructed in shoemaking, an important skill, it turned out, as boots wore out quickly in those days when most travel was on foot. He became quite adept in the craft and this would be put to good use in later times.

The men were astonished when they were informed that they would be paid for their labour! Alas, it was only one-third of a penny per day, an allowance to spend on tobacco from the government store.

A prisoner of the time, James Hardy Vaux*, wrote in later correspondence:

---

* *James Hardy Vaux, a career criminal, was transported to Australia on three separate occasions. His memoir is the first autobiography written in Australia.*

'Every morning at 7 o'clock all the convicts who were capable of work, in fact all who are capable of getting into the boats, is taken ashore. Here they are employed in all sorts of labour, some of it very fatiguing and while so employed each gang of men is watched and directed by a fellow called a guard. These guards are commonly of the lowest class of human beings; wretches devoid of feeling; ignorant in the extreme, brutal by nature, and rendered tyrannical and cruel by the consciousness of the power they possess. They invariably carry a large and ponderous stick, with which, without the slightest provocation, they fell an unfortunate convict to the ground and frequently repeat their blows long after the poor fellow is insensible.'

The standard daily ration for each man was a quarter pound of bread and a quart of thick gruel, twice daily. The weekly ration was a quarter pound of cheese and fourteen ounces raw weight of meat. These meals were served on the deck, with few tables and a handful of seats, forcing many to stand. The rate of mortality on the hulks ranged upwards from five percent, depending on who was counting! The standards of hygiene were so poor that disease spread quickly. It was the practice to sometimes provide the dead with an apparently decent burial. The deceased were placed in a proper coffin and carried to a spot of sands or soil for burial. In practice the coffin had a false, easily removed, bottom and would be re-used often.

Abraham's companions were principally men like him, out of work labourers who had committed crimes that today we regard as petty, probably earning the offender a suspended sentence or twenty hours community work!

Two sixteen-year-old boys shared his cage, each sentenced to seven years transportation for cutting the twine on several bundles of hay. Another lad had been sentenced to seven years for having no visible means of support. Also on the ship were a boy aged only eleven and two aged thirteen. In most cases any transportation sentence meant 'life'. How would these people ever get funds to go home? It is difficult to imagine crimes so serious as to tear boys so young from their homes. As dreadful as conditions were, it should be said that many were little worse off than they were as free people.

Abraham was now firmly a prisoner of the King, denied even the opportunity to say farewell to his mother, family and friends. The cruelty of the law-makers of England toward the poor of the time is hard to surpass.

He was incarcerated in a disgusting hulk on Portsmouth Harbour for several months, separated from his family and his friends for the sake of six halfpennies.

Chapter Three

Hard work. A taste of the lash. The diet. The Britannia *horror. Letters to home. Medical exams. A sea voyage.*

LIFE on a prison hulk. Each day, excepting Sunday of course, as the Sabbath was strictly observed, groups of men chained together were taken to work on the wharves or public works. The brutality of the guards extended to ordering the lash. Twenty-five or even fifty lashes for any insolence or other minor offence was common; Abraham would have witnessed many of these horrors. Taken on deck, the offender was stripped and lashed firmly to a grate. The ship's boatswain was given the honour of administering the first twelve lashes and each subsequent half dozen was given by a different crew member. All prisoners were assembled to witness this as a

Hulks (left) at anchor in the Portsmouth harbour. Artist possibly Garneray. National Maritime Museum, Greenwich, London, Caird Collection

warning to them. Each stroke tore furrows in the flesh and the agony is not hard to imagine. Afterwards the victim was doused heavily in salt water; the salt causing severe pain. The lash left a never fading memory on victim and witness alike.

The food usually served to the prisoners was regarded as adequate by government authorities. At breakfast a wooden tub, known as a kid, was brought to the cages. In the tub lurked a disgusting mess called soup, consisting of barley and tough meat with added salt, boiled for hours. The men ladled as much of it as possible onto their plates and ate. The remaining two daily meals usually contained some sort of boiled, salted meat and barley, with a hunk of black bread. Potatoes were sometimes served, and on three days each week, a small portion of cheese.

Many men died on the hulks, dysentery being the most common cause. The sick were treated to the standard purgatives, bleedings and blisterings, and even in spite of the cure, a number actually managed to survive. Those that didn't were taken ashore by the work gangs and buried, accompanied by a few meaningless words from a preacher

The prisoner Abraham waited apprehensively for news of his transportation. He had heard many dreadful stories, mostly true, of convict ship journeys to Australia and was fearful of what may lie ahead.

One story often repeated concerned the convict ship *Britannia*. She carried 144 men and boys plus forty-four women and girls. Only ninety-four arrived at Port Jackson,

The Hooghly.

many of them in a deplorable state that lead to their deaths soon after. It was a fortunate man who survived the journey, and it was a lucky female indeed, who arrived at Port Jackson without being raped or otherwise molested.

The captain, Thomas Dennot, was a beast. A few days out of port he imagined a planned mutiny and ordered the Irish 'ringleaders' to be punished. One man, James Brennan, received 300 lashes the first day and 500 the next, a staggering 800 lashes which reduced the man to a quivering wreck with his back and buttocks in tatters. He died a few hours after his last flogging. John Bourke received 600 lashes in two sessions and Patrick Garney 400, all at one time. Garney died next day. Cox, Ruttledge and Brady each received 300 strokes of the cat. Yarnley, Stapleton and Garidly, endured 400. All died.

Women had their heads shaved and were placed naked in

head yokes then whipped with canes by Dennot, soldiers or seamen. They were given by Dennot to the troops and seamen as sex slaves. Ninety prisoners died on the voyage, almost all of them victims of Dennot's madness. In spite of complaints to authorities, no action was ever taken against him.

Abraham and his mates all heard similar stories about the *Atlas* horror, the *Hillsborough* and the *Royal Admiral*. All true, and enough to strike fear into any heart.

* * *

On July 25th 1834, the *Hooghly* sailed into Portsmouth, where she commenced to take on board her quota of prisoners. Word had come to Abraham that this ship was to be his conveyance to Port Jackson, and excitement, heavily tinged with fear, ran through him. He could not imagine life on the *Hooghly* being any worse than the hulks

Loaded aboard, the men were told that they could write a farewell letter to family if they wished. Abraham and most of his mates could not read or write, so the offer meant nothing to them. Those who could write received handsome payment from any illiterate men who had some money. Abraham, of course, had none.

On the 26th of July, 1834, a perfect summer day when England was at its most beautiful, the *Hooghly* raised anchor and set sail for Australia.

Their journey was to prove relatively uneventful and without cruel treatment, unlike many others. At this time, the convict ship owners were paid by contract and a typical payment was eighteen pounds per head, plus a bonus of four pounds for every prisoner landed alive. This was an improvement on the earlier system of a flat rate per ton, which meant that there was no incentive to keep prisoners in good health. In fact, the opposite was the case as owners saved money on provisions if captives died. The compulsory appointment of a surgeon on board also helped save lives, but the quality of these men was suspect. The better doctors earned comfortable livings at home, and the men on ships were often drunkards or incompetent or both.

The new system of payment did not, however, prevent unscrupulous ships' captains from withholding food for sale at inflated prices at Port Jackson.

Prior to boarding the *Hooghly*, the men were given a 'medical examination'. In theory, the men judged unfit were excluded from the journey, but it was different in practice. Often the medical men didn't even bother with an examination, instead calling the names and issuing a clean bill of health to all. But even if the doctors had acted properly, most of the men would have concealed any illness simply to escape being returned to the hell of the hulks.

This careless attitude sometimes led to serious contagious diseases being carried onto the ship, with disastrous results. The *Hillsborough* was a dreadful example. Typhoid fever was carried on board and it swept through the passengers. Ninety-five of the 300 convicts on board were dead before the ship arrived at Port Jackson and many more died later. The *Royal Admiral* lost forty-eight to the same disease, one of them Samuel Taylor, the surgeon himself.

The *Hooghly's* journey to Port Jackson was relatively uneventful, with smooth seas and fine weather, but discipline was very strict. On one occasion a man lit a small fire below decks as a prank. He was given a hundred lashes for his trouble. There the incident should have ended, but a man, Clifton, was overheard to say that he wished the whole ship was on fire. As punishment he was ordered to run on deck carrying his straw mattress for two hours. It was very hot – thirty-five degrees – and the poor man eventually collapsed near death. He was fortunate enough to eventually recover.

To the credit of the *Hooghly's* surgeon, he kept a close watch on the issue of provisions, and Abraham and his companions fared much better than many others.

But it was far from paradise. The men were kept below decks for most of the time, six to a cage, and in the tropics it became unbearably hot and stank to high heaven. The men were allowed to wash on deck each day, in seawater bucketed into a large kid, which was a welcome relief.

Crossing the equator relieved the boredom with the traditional celebrations. Fifty of the men were ducked overboard in rope slings. Hauled back on board, several men were stripped of their pants and given a traditional, but painfully rough and undoubtedly terrifying, pubic hair shave with a slashing cut-throat razor. This caused great mirth to the observers but considerable pain and embarrassment to the victims who lay motionless, afraid to twitch even a muscle, during the process.

Chapter Four

Port Jackson and Sydney Town, 1834. The Hooghly. *The marketplace. The people. The convicts. The women.*

NOVEMBER 18th, 1834 was a typically warm and sunny day as the sailing ship *Hooghly*, 113 days out from Portsmouth, dropped anchor in the clear blue waters of Sydney Cove in Port Jackson. On board was her crew of twelve men, skippered by Captain George Bayley, a cluster of perhaps twenty soldiers and 260 convict men.

It was the *Hooghly's* fourth trip to Sydney as a convict transport, her first was in 1825. Others followed in 1828 and 1831. The 1834 journey was to be her last before retiring to coastal service at home. The stoutly built 466 ton timber vessel had established a solid reputation for speedy journeys to Australia, averaging 113 days; quite impressive for a time when 140 days was not uncommon. She also had a reputation for safe arrivals, with total losses of only four convict lives when it was not unusual for a ship to bury thirty or more at sea. On this occasion the *Hooghly* had lost no-one. It had been an excellent, fair weather voyage.

Convicts, crew members and soldiers alike, stood on deck and looked about them toward Sydney Town. The prisoners especially had little idea of what the place was like, or of what lay ahead for them.

On the shore to the north was thick Australian bush, the

dark green, so different to Britain, to which they would become accustomed. To the south, the water stretched to a distant forested shore, too far away to make out any detail. Behind them were the heads, North and South, which guarded the harbour entrance. And ahead was Sydney Town, a bustling waterfront settlement of 16 000 people, around one-half of them convicts or emancipists.

The jetties and wharves were buzzing with activity as ships unloaded their cargoes, much of it produce from the farms of the Parramatta, Hawkesbury and Lane Cove River areas, the food bowl of the colony. Prominent too, were the loads of cedar timber, harvested from the abundant forests to the near north.

Striking features of the men's view were the numerous whirring windmills, the bustling wharves and the large accumulation of impressive sandstone buildings, the latter built by the abundant, hapless convict men, encouraged by the generous use of the lash. The sandstone for the buildings was quarried nearby by other groups of lash-driven labourers.

The previously pristine Tank Stream, which provided the settlement with water, had become an open sewer, discharging its disgusting, germ-laden filth into the harbour. Water carriers prospered at threepence a bucket. Clothing and bodies were foul as many citizens preferred to buy rum rather than wash.

The ground around the harbour was steep and lofty, so the pubs, shops and houses ranged on terraces rather than in streets. The military barracks was a dominant feature, occupying a sweep of land in the town's centre.

Nearby was the town's newly opened marketplace, where settlers sold their fruits, vegetables, crafts and meats. Unloading the horsedrawn drays were the men and women of the poorest class, many of them dressed in the uniform of faded blue cotton, the cheap dungaree* material from India, topped off by straw or kangaroo skin hats. The better-off ridiculed them as the 'dungaree settlers'.

Adjacent to the market were the innumerable hotels and shanties that catered for the proletariat. Foremost among them was the Market House, whose clients included many poor Irish, with some English, and an increasing number of native-born Australians, the 'currency lads' as they were called. A significant number of the poor settlers were emancipated convicts. A large quantity of rum was consumed here, the drink favoured by the poor. It was cheap and plentiful, selling at fifteen pence a half pint! No excise, or even GST!

George Street was the town's principal thoroughfare, running inland from The Rocks at Sydney Cove through the middle of the ground on which the town was built.

In York Street, the soldiers of the 4th and 50th regiments from the barracks carried out noisy daily drills which reverberated across the town. The two regiments were headed by corrupt men who openly enjoyed the privileges of free prostitutes and ready access to convict girls held in the

---

* *Dungaree is the material from which modern day jeans are made.*

upstairs of the barracks in Hyde Street. Other ranks joined in this as well, climbing the walls at night. Soldiers were generally of the lowest types and despised by most residents, many of them shacked up with various 'wives' in their Kent Street quarters.

The military presence was constant. Each evening the air was filled with the sounds of their drums and bugles signalling the end of the convicts' day, with another miserable day to follow.

It was common to see twenty convict men yoked to a wagon loaded with gravel, stone or timber, supplying the teams who built the roads and bridges. Such men were treated worse than animals.

For the convict women it was hell. On arrival they were promptly sent to the Female Factory to become engaged in spinning yarn or weaving cloth. They had babies galore, primarily fathered by soldiers who had free and unlimited access to them. On regular occasions, the women were paraded for settlers to choose a wife – often to be used as a prostitute, easy money for the man. The serious lack of females in the colony saw homosexuality flourish and ill-concealed auto-sexual practices among the men abounded. Free and emancipated women, not uncommonly treated as chattels, frequently had little choice than to become prostitutes or thieves to survive.

In the yard of the jail the gallows were in full public view, with hangings so common as to attract little public interest. Sometimes multiple hangings drew a small crowd and a

The Pure Merino of New South Wales by S.T. Gill, *courtesy of John Tully.*

favourite gambling pastime saw bets placed on whether the hanged would defecate on death. Odds were about fifty-fifty.

Convicts being 'married to the three sisters' were common. This was a local term for being tied to the triangle for flogging.

Fifty thousand lashes was the official flogging figure for Sydney in the year 1834, but it was in fact a lot more. The floggings were administered by scourgers, usually sadistic former convicts, who were paid eight pence a day more than a constable! The cruellest punishment, the treadmill, was in constant use.

This then was Sydney as Abraham Braybrook first saw it in November 1834. It was populated by a motley collection of farmers, soldiers, convicts, businessmen, publicans, labourers, tradesmen, servants, prostitutes, Aboriginals and drunks, and of course, the self-styled aristocrats and gentry, commonly known locally as the 'pure merinos'.

This was the Australia that was to become home for the convict men aboard the *Hooghly*. Most of them never returned to their homelands and their families.

Chapter Five

Governor Bourke. The arrival. The sea voyage. Inworth Village, Essex. Harsh U.K. laws. Unemployment. Chartists-Unions. Tolpuddle martyrs. A brush with the law.

IN 1834, the colony of New South Wales was controlled by Governor Richard Bourke, a compassionate and progressive man, who contrasted with most of those before him and those around him. Governor Arthur in Van Diemans' Land, for example, oversaw a reign of terror, and he regularly sent men to Port Arthur if they didn't respond to his ghastly 'cures'.

Governor Bourke was a true liberal whose vision for Australia went beyond a dumping ground for convicts, the unwanted people of the United Kingdom. He saw it as a potentially prosperous and free land, a jewel in the crown of the British Empire. He opposed the methods of control used against the convict population, the lash in particular. He even proposed to his masters in England that no more convicts be transported, an appeal that was firmly rejected. Those beside him, the pure merinos and exclusives resented his liberal outlook and he became increasingly isolated from the most powerful citizens. This led to his eventual recall to England.

Imposing church buildings dominated the streetscape of Sydney where Christianity was a strong force. Regrettably, the church leaders had little care or understanding for the wretched convicts and emancipists, instead focusing on the free and wealthy, condoning the flogging, the torture and the inhumanity. Not surprisingly, most convicts turned away from the church on their release, frequently describing the clergy as sanctimonious mongrels and hypocrites. There were many dreadful acts carried out under the cloak of the Christian religion. George Loveless, one of the pathetic Tolpuddle Martyrs, famously said: 'From religion such as this, deliver us Oh Lord'. He later told of a starving, beaten fellow prisoner who pleaded for food from a visiting clergyman. Instead of food, the minister delivered to him a bible and prayer book. There is more about Tolpuddle later.

It seems that the main achievement of the churchmen of New South Wales was the rigorous enforcement of the observance of the Sabbath.

On board the *Hooghly*, Abraham Braybrook, the 23-year-old from Kelvedon, Essex (according to 'All Saints' Great Braxted church records, he was christened on July 17th, 1811), shared the apprehension of his travelling companions; anxious and fearful of the unknown that lay ahead. He and his companions were given no indication of the next step and were completely at the mercy of their captors.

A longboat of officials, accompanied by a handful of soldiers, drew alongside the anchored vessel and they ascended the rope ladders slung over the ship's side. The longboat had towed a small barge, and from it, vast bundles of clothing were hauled on board. The convicts were lined up on the deck and ordered to strip naked, bundling their filthy clothing to hand over to collecting soldiers. Large wooden tubs were filled with harbour water and the men ordered to bathe, six to a tub. The bath completed they were told to stand at attention in the sun until they dried. No place for modesty here as some sneering military men made fun of their unaccustomed nakedness.

The men were handed their new clothes; dull grey combined with bright yellow trousers and jackets, a pair of boots, stockings, shirts and hats. Much of the outer clothing bore the broad arrow stamp we associate with the convict uniform of the time. The bright yellow was the reason for the popular use of 'canary' when people spoke of convicts.

Each man was called forward for recording of identification details before dressing and boarding the boat for ferrying to the jetty. The number 2480 was called by the soldier in charge and Abraham stepped forward. He was questioned about his religious beliefs and was noted in the record as a Protestant.

The officer wrote other details: hair fair, complexion ruddy, scar over left eye, eyes grey. He measured Abraham's height, tall for the times at five feet, nine and a half inches. Abraham was then ordered to sign the document, making the customary X of those who were illiterate, before being told to dress and board the longboat.

It was almost dark by the time all the men were assembled on shore and marched to the overcrowded convict barracks.

Here they were each handed a blanket and a bowl of soup with a thick slice of bread. The barracks, completed in 1819 and housing 580 men, was still comparatively new and an improvement on the previous accommodation system for convicts. Before the barracks opened, each convict had been responsible for finding their own accommodation, paid for by the authorities, but deducted from their minuscule pay in government service. This meant that the best available to them was undoubtedly squalid.

After the meagre meal in the falling darkness they were ordered to bed. The cots were hard, smelly and damp, but several months of incarceration on the hulk *Leviathan* in Portsmouth harbour and the long journey on the *Hooghly* had accustomed Abraham and his companions to this type of treatment. Sleeping with stink and filth now came easy to Abraham Braybrook.

I digress now, but it is an important subject for all who cherish liberty. In 1834 the Chartist rebellion, the forerunner of our Trade Unions, was gathering strength. The yielding to civilised feeling was, however, still a long way off, uncivilised practices still abounded. Branding with hot irons was still practiced and gibbeting was not yet abolished, but was soon to be. Gibbeting involves publicly suspending the rotting body of a hanged person for a week or more and was said to be a deterrent to crime.

The ghastly practice of drawing and quartering for

extremely serious crimes had only recently been done away with. Such inhumanity is hard to imagine. Dear reader, you may find this description disgusting, but it is accurate. You may wish to skip the next paragraph.

The condemned man would be sentenced to the short drop method of hanging, so that the neck would not break. The man was usually dragged half alive to the quartering table where he was awakened, if unconscious, as he was laid down on the table. A large cut was made in the gut after cutting off the penis and testicles. Then the intestines would be dragged out one by. Each piece of organ would be burned before the sufferer's eyes, and when he was completely disembowelled, his head would be cut off. The body would then be cut into four pieces. The five parts of the body were then put on public display in various parts of the country. Thankfully this punishment was never used in Australia. They were harsh times indeed in dear old England; the Mother Country some call it. Spare us all from mothers like that!

As mentioned, the trade union movement was in its beginnings in the middle of the 19th century, around the time of Abraham's exit to Australia. The hierarchy, who feared the power of men united and saw unions as a threat to exploitation and profit, promptly outlawed it. Even today, determined attempts are made to disempower some unions, but surely they will remain while at least some workers remain loyal and true to each other.

An unhappy example of discriminatory punishment for any persons then thinking of workers' unity concerned the famed Tolpuddle Martyrs. Tolpuddle was a small village in Dorset where, one evening, six men met to discuss ideas and details in their attempt to form a union. The men had just experienced a cut in pay from nine shillings a week to six shillings, a pittance that could not feed their families.

The six were arrested, charged with sedition and sentenced to terms of transportation to Australia ranging from seven years to life.

In Australia, one of the men, George Loveless, stated to authorities that he had committed no crime and for this impudence was sent to work on the dreaded chain gang – a life not fit for dogs. In gangs of eight, chained by the legs, the men toiled daylight to dark on backbreaking work on the roads and other public works. Often there was bedding for only half of the group in their crude mobile hut; they took turns to sleep on the dirty and often damp floor.

In 1836, following continuing outrage and protests in England, the Tolpuddle Six were pardoned and allowed to return to their homes and families.

Chapter Six

*Henry Boucher Bowerman. 'Marion'. Parramatta.
Murder, bloody murder! Lerida Creek. William Allen.
23 servants. Bombala – The High Country. Assembly at Yass.*

ABRAHAM's concerns about his future soon ended when an ambitious gentleman, Henry Boucher Bowerman visited the barracks. Bowerman is important to this story because of his involvement in Abraham's future adventures.

He was on a mission to select men to serve him on his 130 acre farm Marion situated on the northern bank of the Parramatta River, part of the Field of Mars. One of the men chosen from a line-up was Abraham due to his strong appearance and past farming experience

Governor Arthur Phillip had named the district The Field of Mars when he granted land there to eight military men in 1792 – Mars being the ancient Roman God of War. Governor Phillip believed the name reflected the military association of the eight new settlers on that land. One of them was Alexander McDonald. On his death, his widow had sold part of the property to E.B. Miller who built the home named Rose Farm. In 2007, my wife Marilyn and I visited that house which still stands in what is now 15–17 Honor Street, Ermington. It was in poor condition, obviously neglected, but it remains to this day.

The remainder of the McDonald property was later

purchased by Bowerman where he began to grow fruit and vegetables to supply a hungry Sydney Town. He named the property Marion for his wife and built a large home, Broadoaks, which was due west of the current Rydalmere Public School

In 1945, the Field of Mars was acquired by the federal government for the development of social housing, and hundreds of homes were built for returned servicemen and their families. The remainder became, and remains, a community reserve and cemetery. Broadoaks was demolished in 1950 to make way for more Housing Commission homes. A road in Ermington is named for it.

An interesting aside tells us that the well known Kissing Point got it's name from heavily laden ships entering the Parramatta River often bumping into rocks protruding into the river, that is, kissing the rocks. Hence, Kissing Point. There is no reason to doubt this

E.B. Miller built Rose Farm. It is now 15–17 Honor Street, Ermington.

Henry Boucher Bowerman was a military man, appointed to Moreton Bay (now Brisbane), in charge of the explosives and powder magazine, a relatively high rank. Previously he had served briefly at Port Macquarie penal settlement where seven hundred men were held captive in dreadful conditions. Around 1834 he was transferred as Officer in Charge of Magazines (explosives stores) at Parramatta.

Bowerman had studied at the Woolwich, UK, Military Academy where he also learnt the art of drawing and painting. He produced some excellent works, including two early sketches of Moreton Bay held in the State Library of Queensland. They are believed to be the earliest pictorial views of Brisbane, circa 1831. He came to Australia with his wife Marion on the *Grenada*, arriving in 1825.

Bowerman had no justifiable use for a large company of servants at Marion, but he had other plans, the success of which greatly depended on his having abundant and free labour. Convicts were a real bargain for the 'right people' and the wealthy. Convicts cheap to maintain? You bet! The standard weekly ration for convict servants was set down by the authorities. It consisted of eight pounds of meat per week, one ounce of tea and a couple of pounds of flour. Potatoes and other vegetables were issued frugally in season. Good slave masters also issued a few ounces of tobacco, often grown on the property to extract the nicotine for sheep dip.

When Henry Bowerman retired after twenty-two years of military service, he was awarded a retirement entitlement; a very generous remission of one hundred and fifty pounds on any government land purchase. As well, he was entitled to a military pension fixed at half his salary for life.

The military-man/farmer was pleased to select Abraham for service, especially when he learned of his bootmaking skill. He signed the necessary papers, and together with ten other chosen convicts, Abraham was walked the entire distance to Marion to begin work. It was to be little more than a staging station as it turned out. Bowerman, was thinking well ahead and his plans extended far beyond Marion and Parramatta,

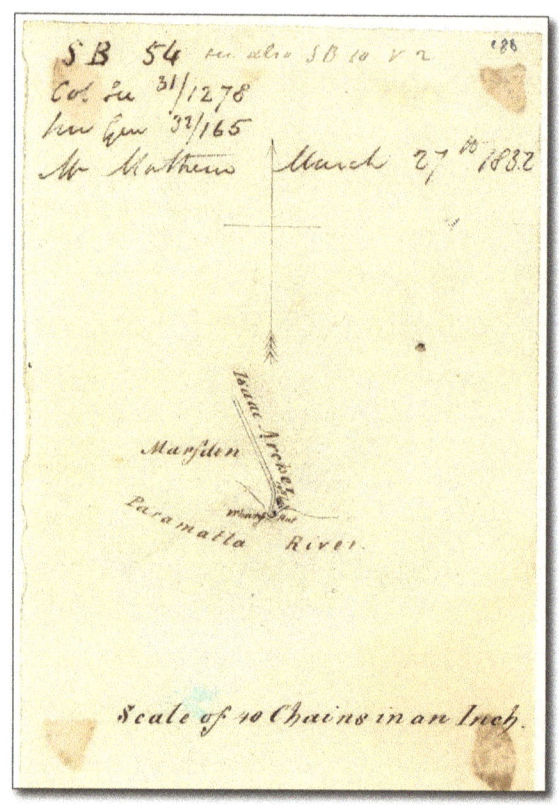

Copy of the land survey sketch, Archer and Marsden, Field Of Mars, Parramatta. Library of NSW.

his intention being to become a well-off landholder, one of the gentry. He had already been involved in considerable land speculation and was prospering as a result.

There was a noteworthy incident on record which took place at Marion about a month after Abraham and John Davis arrived there. It occurred shortly before they and a man named Budge left there for Lerida and the Monaro Plains. There was a ghastly murder of one of the workers! Even though violence was common enough, this was high drama at the time.

The farm workers shared accommodation in the form of rough huts. Each was shared by two and sometimes three men. One morning, a man named James Taylor called on his mates Johnny Devine and Henry Higgins who shared a hut with William Coffee. Coffee's hut was about a hundred yards from the hut Abraham shared with John Davis. The previous evening, Taylor had spent many hours consuming copious quantities of rum with his friends and a John Jenkins. On entering the hut next morning, he was horrified to see the drinking companion, John Jenkins, lying on the floor in a pool of blood, his throat had been cut.

Military men were quickly called to investigate, but oddly nobody was charged with the obvious murder. It appeared a drunken fight may have gotten out of control with disastrous results. Soon after this, Davis, Budge and Abraham left Marion for Lerida and put the incident behind them.

* * *

In 1835, using his retirement discount entitlement, Bowerman purchased two blocks, each of six hundred and forty acres, at Lerida Creek, a locality between Gunning and Collector, about 25 miles east of Yass. At a mere three hundred and twenty pounds (five shillings an acre), less discounts, it was a splendid bargain. Clever finance man that he was, he somehow managed to stock it with seven thousand sheep – overstocked of course – but as we will see, he had far more expansive plans. He soon moved his goods and servants to Lerida Creek where a station was established.

As his Lerida property was within the acknowledged 'settled district', he was entitled to have numerous assigned convict servants. Calculated on the amount of livestock he owned, he was entitled to twenty-three assigned servants, which he quickly gained. It is rarely properly acknowledged

Pencil drawing of Moreton Bay (Brisbane) c.1835 by Henry Bowerman, believed to be the oldest picture of Brisbane in existence (Museum of Queensland).

Map showing the location of Lerida. Google Maps.

that this country was built on the sweat and pain of hapless convicts. What was fundamentally ownership of convicts made life much easier for the well off and at absolute minimal cost.

In 1836, Henry Bowerman engaged a free man, William Allen, to be his overseer on these properties and despatched him southward to Lerida with a good number of his charges.

Allen, about thirty years old, was a hard master and extracted every ounce of effort from his prisoners, under threat of taking them before a magistrate if they were insolent or lazy. They had no doubts about the type of punishment. The magistrates, always district squatters, dispensed fifty to a hundred lashes without fail.

Previously, Bowerman had negotiated to take over the lease of James Atkinson, who held Aston station in the Monaro district of the Snowy Mountains. The lease included 200 head of cattle, all to be sold at bargain prices, as Atkinson was keen to return to England and was open to any reasonable offer. Bowerman was a ruthless businessman and did not let the opportunity pass him by. His principal objective of course was to obtain the cattle. He soon sent the orders to William Allen to journey to Aston to round up the cattle and bring them to Lerida.

Perusal of the daily roll call of servants at Lerida at this time shows that Abraham, Budge and John Davis were not included. These roll calls were strictly conducted and any missing person would certainly have been pursued and reported to authorities.

Their absence showed that they had been selected by William Allen to accompany him on this journey, travelling south from Lerida to Aston. We know that this is correct as it was later revealed in the trial which resulted from the murder at Marion, during which Abraham stated to the court that he remembered going to the Monaro Plains and had discussions with Budge at the time concerning the murder.

Allen was mounted on a fine horse. Budge, Davis and Abraham either shared another horse that was required for the round up at the station, or they took turns driving a horse and dray loaded with supplies.

It was a gruelling, exhausting 120 mile (180 kilometre) trek from Lerida to Aston which was between Cooma and Bombala, close to the present-day New South Wales–Victoria border. Their route was defined by a faintly blazed track through thick bush; blazed by Johann Lhotsky in 1834. Lhotsky was an amateur explorer who set out from Yass in February equipped with one horse and cart and four servants. He arrived at the present day site of Cooma

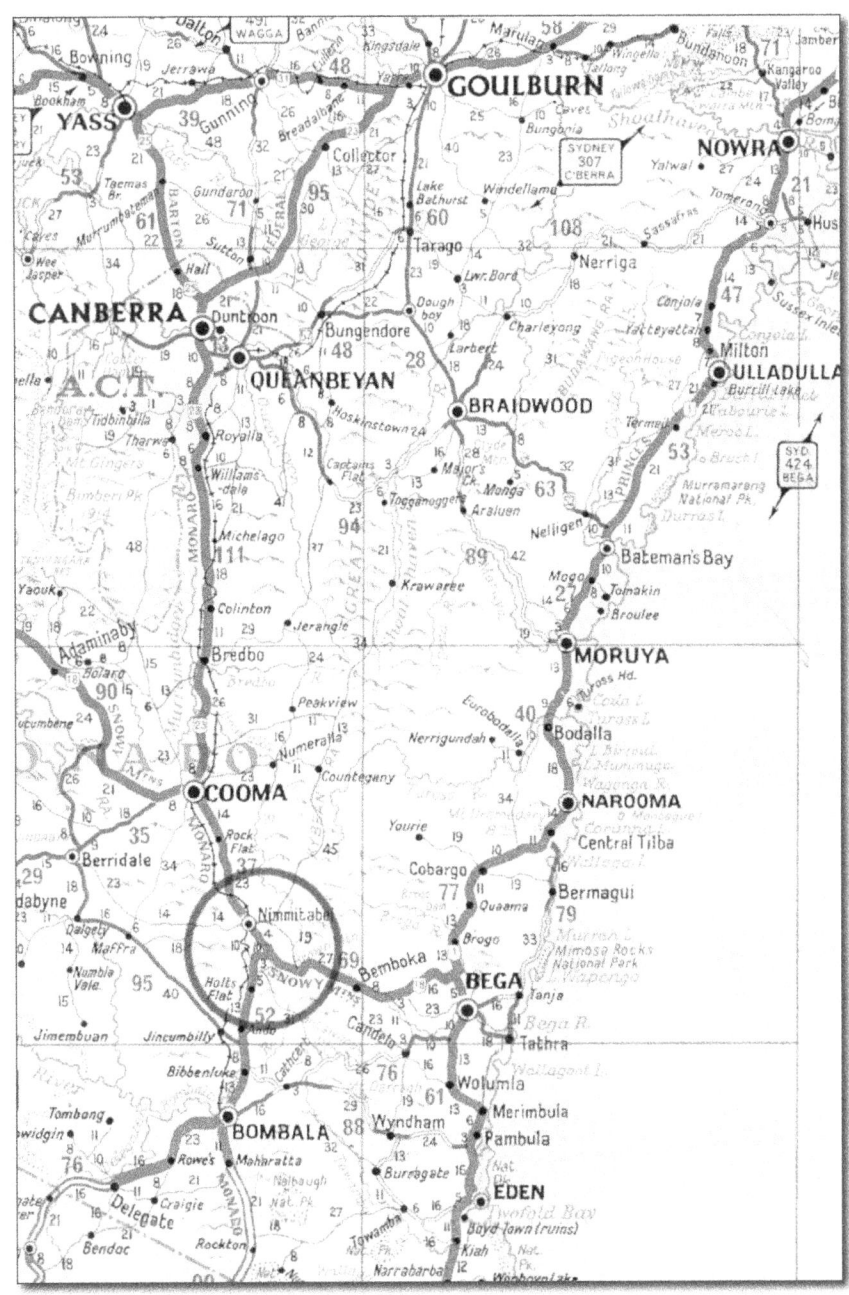

Circled is the approximate location of Aston Station on the Monaro Plains.

and continued west until fierce weather forced him back, however, not before he viewed 'luxuriant alpine meadows' – probably the Monaro* Plains. His trail, now being followed by the Allen party, was compounded by the hoofs of many cattle, made by Atkinson and his group a year before.

Marathon journeys such as this were not common, not even then. Abraham Braybrook, Henry Budge and John Davis were, therefore, among the very earliest white men to venture into what ranks as the wildest and most hostile country in Australia. But you won't find their names in any history books.

Davis and Abraham in particular were to become good mates, destined to share many adventures.

Accommodation at the site was a couple of canvas tents – a typically rough camp. The convicts were given considerable freedom to roam, confident that there could be no attempt to abscond. The work was hard, and the isolation we can only imagine. It would take some days to round up all the stock from such a large, unfenced area, although cattle instinctively live in herds. It was a matter of locating some and the rest would be nearby.

* * *

---

* *William Wells described the Monaro Plains in 1848 as: "a series of undulations, soil is rich and fertile, forming a square about 100 miles in extent – larger pasture than the whole of Tasmania – 2000 to 3000 feet above sea level – parallel to the coast." The plains are located approximately midway between Cooma and Bombala.*

Back at Parramatta after the Monaro Plains trip, a trial was eventually being held to judge the guilt or innocence of the suspected murderers of John Jenkins – William Coffee, John Devine and Patrick Higgins. Due to the close proximity of their hut, Abraham and John Davis were called back from Lerida to give evidence.

They claimed that they had been totally unaware of what had taken place that night; this was the truth. They had spent several hours consuming grog with the group that night, but when they left at about ten o'clock all was well.

We know from court records that Budge would often talk about the murder and a reward. Abraham revealed this when questioned at the trial. He said to the court:

> 'I remember going to Monaro Plains, we started on a Tuesday; Budge went with us; as we went up the country Budge talked about the murder and a reward. He said, "If you and I knew anything about the murder we should get a free pardon."
>
> 'At a river we had sat down to take refreshment and Budge said. "If you and I were to swear that Higgins and little Johnny (Devine) had done this murder, who could say it wasn't true?" I said I would do no such thing. I would rather work in irons, during my sentence. He told different people about the murder on the road. About four or five days after we got to

Monaro Plains, Budge told me that he knew something about the murder; it was in the morning, he got up before I was awake. When I awoke I called him and he did not answer. I went to look for him, he was walking up and down and said, "I can't rest". I asked him what was the matter? He again said, "I can't rest about that murder at Parramatta." I said, "What makes you worry about that, you know nothing about it"; he said "I know more about it than you think." I asked him what he knew, that was all he told me; he went away that day.'

The murder trial went for a full two days (unusual even for a murder trial in those days). Despite damning evidence from Budge, who claimed he had actually witnessed Higgins cut Jenkins' throat as he was held down by the other two, the jury rather astonishingly, found them not guilty.*

On eventual arrival at Lerida, the cattle from Aston had been added to the drive northward to Yass. Arriving at Yass, they found that Bowerman had assembled some 7 000 sheep, including forty-eight merino rams of the famed Macarthur flock. With the addition of the stock from Aston, he now had over 200 head of cattle as well. How he financed the purchase of so much stock is not known, but he was a clever businessman.

---

* *A full report of the trial can be found in* The Sydney Gazette and New South Wales Advertiser, *18 August, 1835 Pp 2 & 3.*

> Abraham Braybrook—I am an assigned servant to Mr. Bowerman; I remember going to Menaro Plains; we started on a Tuesday; Budge went with me; we called at a hut in our way to meet the drays, and saw a young man there (the witness here identified Phillips as the person); we remained there about an hour and three-quarters (this witness corroborated the evidence of Phillips as to the conversation which took place in the hut with respect to the murder); as we went up the country, Budge talked about the murder and the reward; he said, before we got to Parramatta—"If you or I knew any thing about the murder we should get a free pardon;" when Murrumbidgee River we sat down to take some refreshment, and Budge said, "If you and I were to swear that Higgins and little Johnny (Devine) had done this murder, who could contradict us?" I said, ' I will do no such thing I would rather work in irons during my sentence;" he told different people about the murder on the road; about four or five days after we got to Menaro Plains, Budge told me he knew something about the murder; it was in the morning; he got up before I was awake; when I awoke I called him, and as he did not answer I went out to look after him; he was walking up and down, and said, "I can't rest;" I asked what was the matter; he again said, "I can't rest about that murder at Parramatta; I said what makes you uneasy about that, you know nothing about it; he said, " I know more about it than you think for;" I asked him what he knew (the witness here related the circumstance about the trousers); that was all he told me; he went away that day.

Extract from The Sydney Gazette and New South Wales Advertiser, *18 August, 1835 reporting the trial.*

Major Thomas Mitchell, a good friend to Bowerman, had returned from his journey of exploration into what he called *Australia Felix**, with glowing reports of the great land available there for the taking. He told his friend Bowerman of it, and he acted without hesitation.

He decided to surrender his current leaseholds and go south to *Australia Felix*, taking all his stock, his overseer and, against the law, all twenty-three assigned convicts. Note that convicts were not permitted outside 'the settled areas'.

---

* *Major Thomas Mitchell named much of the region south of the Murray River* Australia Felix *(including the Alps which he did not explore) to distinguish it from the more barren lands he and others had explored to the north.* Felix *is Latin for lucky, successful, implying fruitful, productive, fertile etc.*

Bowerman wouldn't undertake the overland journey himself, possibly because it was likely to be dangerous and certainly strenuous and uncomfortable. Instead, he appointed William Allen to lead the trek overland and to make a preliminary selection of quality land in his name on arrival at a suitable destination. He had set his sights on an area that Mitchell had told him was 'a valley of the finest description'. Bowerman would join them later, making the journey by ship to Port Phillip in relative comfort and at far greater speed. There he would meet Allen and go by horseback to the preliminary land choice made by his overseer and make a final decision. By the middle of 1837, all was in readiness for a departure.

Chapter Seven

Abraham's overland journey to Australia Felix *begins.
Leaving Yass. Yaldwyn, Brown and Allen.*

BOWERMAN'S party was not alone in its intention to leave Yass for the new land. Also assembled were two other groups, one headed by the aristocratic William Yaldwyn and the other by an old sea-dog, Captain John Sylvester Brown, nicknamed Paddy because of his Irish blood.

Yaldwyn had stolen the march on others who sought what amounted to virtually free land. He had already sent his man, John Coppock, ahead with a small party to select a station for him, aware that the first arrivals would secure the best lands. In July, 1837, he chose a magnificent 60 000 acres on the Campaspe River, for which Yaldwyn paid just ten pounds a year rent to the Crown. Paradoxically, fourteen years later, men had to pay almost twice that for a license to earn a living by digging for gold, but that's another story.

Henry Bowerman, not one who relished the rugged life, had already decided to make the journey by ship to Port Phillip, then by horseback to his new lands with his overseer William Allen.

Yass was only a small village at the time – perhaps fifty people – established to serve the handful of settlers who had taken up the fine land in the area. The frantic activity must have greatly impressed the locals, as thousands of sheep and hundreds of cattle were herded on its outskirts. The solitary pub did a roaring trade.

The three groups decided to travel in a loose convoy; Yaldwyn moving out first, followed by William Allen and to the rear came Captain Brown. They would follow 'the Major's line', the trail blazed by Major Thomas Mitchell's party as it returned from the Portland district to Sydney.

William Allen's group was undoubtedly the most impressive, with several large drays, a boat wagon drawn by bullocks, seven thousand sheep, two hundred cattle and several horses. There were the twenty-three convict workers, mostly sheep and cattle herders, and several free men, principally bullock drivers. Abraham by this time had established himself with Allen as reliable and trustworthy and was well regarded.

The other two parties were similar, but smaller in

The picturesque Yass Valley in NSW.
(picture: canberraregiontablelands.com)

number. A notable difference was the horsedrawn caravan accommodation provided for William Yaldwyn, not one to sacrifice too many of life's little luxuries!

What a great journey lay ahead! They were already over 125 miles (200 kilometres) from civilised Sydney, and ahead was 400 miles (650 kilometres) across virtually unexplored country, populated by wild Aborigines who were, at the time, believed by many to be belligerent and even cannibals. There were many rivers to cross and hills to climb, hard miles to walk or to ride and dangers at every turn. Their route would take them through or near the present day towns of Jugiong, Gundagai, Tarcutta, Holbrook, Albury, Howlong, Wangaratta, Benalla, Heathcote, Newstead and Castlemaine.

Again, the courage of men like Abraham Braybrook braving the unknown and the isolation must be admired, even though it was forced upon them. The alternative was to refuse to go, with a consequent date with the lash, topped by an enduring term on dreaded Norfolk Island.

At 7 am on Monday October 23rd, 1837, the Yaldwyn party said goodbye to Yass and headed south. Most of the district population had heard of the ventures and came for a look. The three departures were quite an event. Wanting to put a good space between the outfits, Allen decided to hold off until the next day. Captain Brown agreed to do likewise after the Allen party moved off.

Thus, in the early morning of October 24th, 1837, Abraham Braybrook's great overland adventure, with the ensuing remarkable events, began.

Chapter Eight

*The Murrumbidgee River. Tarcutta to Billabong Creek.
Seven Mile Creek. Hot weather. Dead men's bones.
Cannibals? The Murray River. Rest days.*

SOME of the following detail is gleaned from a study of J.O. Randell's excellent account of William Yaldwyn's journey south, *Yaldwyn of the Golden Spurs*, and this is readily acknowledged. Abraham's party would have shared very similar experiences, as the two groups were only ever a day or two apart.

This rugged land was still strange to Abraham, and he shared the apprehension of most of the party as they prepared to leave Yass, but at least he and Davis had their Monaro experiences to draw on. There was little about the coming journey that resembled life at home in Essex, or even Parramatta. His thoughts would certainly have flown to his home, his mother and all things familiar to him. How was his mother coping? What lay ahead of him?

William Allen was a hard master, and Abraham knew he was in for a rough time. Allen had made it very plain that any bad behaviour or disobedience would be treated with the lash. Even worse, any offender could be sent back to Sydney, which meant being sentenced to the dreaded Norfolk Island convict establishment. Everyone was well aware of how convicts were treated there.

There was considerable fear of Aborigines. Many believed that they were cannibals.

In some ways, however, Allen was not so bad. He broke out rum for the men each night and issued as much tobacco as each man needed. The food was good, too, 'tucker' as it became known, a title that newcomers found quite strange.

Allen constantly worried about Aborigines attacking the party and was in fact almost obsessively hateful of them. In truth, he feared them and passed this fear on to his men with assurances that 'the Blacks will kill you and then eat you'. There was a strong belief in those early days that the Aboriginals were cannibals.

The travellers made a good start southward, following the trail of Yaldwyn and his group, whose party stayed ahead of them for most of the trip. This suited Allen who told Abraham that Yaldwyn was a 'bloody pure merino', a wealthy gentleman, far too good for the likes of him.

Abraham's job was to keep a close watch on the sheep

The Murrumbidgee River near Gundagai. By Bidgie Own Work.

when on the march; to help herd them inside protective hurdles at night, ensuring that the animals did not scatter, especially when wild dogs came around. Each shepherd had about a thousand sheep in his care. These men had the service of Abraham as hutkeeper who cooked for them and lit fires at each camp. The shepherds slept each night in a watch-box – a bed enclosed in a large portable box with a lift up lid. Abraham camped in a tent, where at night he worked at making and repairing boots for the travellers. He kept beside him at all times two fully loaded fowling pieces to shoot marauding dogs and, on Allen's orders, any Aborigines that looked threatening – Blackfellers as they were commonly called. Abraham shot several wild dogs on the journey but, to his undoubted relief, he had no need to shoot any 'Blackfellers'.

The first day out, the party headed north-west toward Flinter's Forge (now Bowning), having crossed the Yass River without difficulty. After an overnight camp they moved directly west to Jugiong Creek, taking this roundabout route to avoid crossing the Murrumbidgee River, but eventually it had to be crossed anyway.

On Sunday the 30th of October they arrived at the banks of this great river at what is the present day town of Gundagai. There the party came upon William Yaldwyn's group which was having difficulty crossing the river. It was wide and swift here with some very deep holes. William Allen was pleased to be able to help Yaldwyn. Together the combined group ferried across about two thousand of Yaldwyn's sheep in the boat and the drays.

It was a major effort, and Allen decided to call a halt for the rest of the day and to proceed the next day. The experience with Yaldwyn's stock was useful to Allen and prompted him to swim the cattle and most of the sheep across, but wisely placed the older ewes in the boat. Numerous trips back and forth were needed for this, but eventually the crossing was completed. Surprisingly, there were few animals lost.

The carts and drays were drawn over by the bullocks and horses without incident. Apart from a good soaking, no member of Abraham's group was worse for wear for their effort.

In the meantime, Captain Paddy Brown's party had crossed the river further north and now led the convoy. This was of no concern as there was no rivalry between the groups.

The next couple of days were uneventful, and by November 2nd they had arrived at Tarquetta Creek (now Tarcutta), which they crossed with relative ease. By November 4th they were at Kiamba Creek; almost twenty miles had been covered in the two days. On the way they overtook Brown's party which had stopped to spell the livestock, but still ahead was William Yaldwyn's party.

The next day they were greeted by Father John Therry at his station, Billabong, which the man of God had settled on some months before. Billabong station was near what is now Holbrook.

By the 7th of November, the group had made it to Seven Mile Creek, where they camped for a further day to rest the stock and allow the men to rest and wash their clothes.

A group of four rough looking men came into the camp in the afternoon and Allen at first took them to be bushrangers, but they were merely looking for a meal as they made their way to Yass for supplies. Allen took the opportunity to despatch with them a letter to Henry Bowerman, to inform him of their progress. By now, Bowerman was back at Parramatta, but the letter was eventually delivered.

The weather had become hot, and early morning starts were the order of the day. The early start was not out of Allen's concern for the welfare of his men, but he was very aware of the welfare of the stock in his care. It was paramount, he was paid the excellent sum of fifty pounds a year for his work and took the responsibility very seriously. By comparison, his bullock drivers received twenty-five pounds and of course the convicts received nought.

Allen teamed Abraham with John Davis and a young lad named Denis Brennan, whom they nicknamed Billy. Billy was serving seven years for some minor offence. Davis was also serving seven years. The three got on well together.

By one o'clock, dinner time, on that day, the drovers arrived at a small creek with good water, and even though they had journeyed only five miles, Allen ordered a stopover. The old ewes especially were extremely distressed by the one hundred degree (Fahrenheit) heat.

The next day was another hot one, again over the century mark, but they had to cover twelve miles before coming to water holes around a large swamp. Toward evening, Allen rode forward, as they were on Mullengandra station, owned by Mister Hutton, and he dined with him.

Whenever he was absent, Allen left James Oliver in charge. Oliver was a free man appointed as Assistant Overseer on a thirty pounds per year salary.

The following day, after covering eleven miles, the party passed through the station recently abandoned by Mister Ebden. He had departed for *Australia Felix* as well.

There was little water there for the stock, so the stay was brief. Allen ordered a return to travel, even though all were exhausted. He was doubly anxious to clear the area as one of Yaldwyn's men had that day found the bones of two white men who had disappeared a few weeks before. It was believed that they had been slain by Aborigines and Allen was convinced that they had been eaten. He urged the men to hurry on unless they wanted to be the next meal*. They needed little urging and slept that night with one eye open.

By Friday the 10th of November, 1837, the party reached the Hume River (now the Murray) at Howlong, just west of what is Albury today. The river here was very wide, much wider than the Murrumbidgee which they had been told was the widest. Allen selected a spot to cross which looked formidable, being almost 100 yards (80 metres) wide. However, he had tested it on horseback and it was no more than five feet deep (1.4 metres) at worst and safe to cross with care. It was a very sultry day again, and the men, and probably the animals, welcomed a dip in the cool water as first the cattle, followed by the younger sheep were swum over, without loss. The precious rams, the future of the flock and therefore the venture, were far too valuable to risk losing, so were boated across, as were the old ewes and the lambs. The crossing was made with the loss of only a few sheep and one cow; considered a good result under the circumstances.

The party camped overnight, and in the morning, swam the working bullocks and the horses across, without event. They rested the remainder of the day. Next day, they proceeded only three miles before stopping again, mostly to rest the ewes and lambs which were travelling very slowly

---

* *Allen's fears may have been well founded. About four months later, a party led by William and George Faithful was attacked by about twenty natives, and eight white men were murdered. One Aboriginal also died.*

and were obviously quite exhausted.

They didn't travel at all the next day, as Allen decided to let the ewes rest some more, a wise decision since there was a long way yet to go. During the stop, the men rounded up the lambs and cut off their tails and their testicles. Abraham had seen this done before back home, and his knowledge in instructing the men was welcomed by Allen. The party was camped on Indigo Creek, which was almost dry, with a mere trickle of water flowing.

All the country around was unimpressive and of the worst description – 'horrid' was William Allen's description.

Chapter Nine

*The Ovens River. The Broken River. The Goulburn River.
John Coppock. The Coliban River. Alexander Mollison.
Charles Ebden. Forest Creek. Expedition Pass. Castlemaine.
A valley of the finest description.*

SATURDAY the 18th of November, 1837, three years to the day since Abraham's arrival in Sydney, was a glorious day, reaching seventy degrees (25°C).

The party made excellent progress toward the Ovens River. On arrival there late in the afternoon they found it was much more challenging than they had imagined. Apparently heavy rains upstream had turned the normally placid stream into a fast flowing river, quite deep in parts and about fifty yards wide (45 metres).

William Allen was perplexed and rode for several miles in either direction looking for a better crossing. He found none and decided to camp the night and try the crossing next morning. Yaldwyn had crossed safely the day before, demonstrating to Allen that it could be done. Captain Paddy Brown was three days behind, and the men had not seen or heard anything of that party for some time.

At dawn next day, even though it was the Sabbath, the work of crossing the river began. First, the cattle were swum across, with the loss of several that could not withstand the current. The younger sheep followed and Abraham marvelled at their strength as they swam strongly through the surging water. An unknown number of them failed to make it, but Allen was well satisfied with the result. Next, the rams, older ewes and the smaller lambs were ferried over in the boat, a time consuming job, but again successful. The drays, still fully laden, were then driven across, and it was breathtaking to see the huge bullocks swim so strongly, dragging the drays behind them to land in safety on the far side. The horses, with riders, crossed the river with relative ease. It was an exhausting time for all involved, and Allen called a halt for the rest of the day and the one following.

It was Wednesday November 22nd when the party came to the Swampy River (now the Broken River), near present day Benalla. At that time of year it was a chain of large billabongs, with the stream itself only about one foot deep (30 mm), and it was crossed with ease. They continued on till they came to a small, unnamed creek which had abundant clear water where they made camp. Next day was extremely hot and windy and they proceeded without incident to another small stream, mostly comprised of muddy waterholes, obviously disturbed by Yaldwyn's stock. Here, Allen called another day of rest for the sheep. The water was barely sufficient, but the heat prevented any attempt to move further.

On Monday the 27th, the heat continued, and the team was weary as it approached what was believed to be the Goulburn River. Alas, it was nothing more than a string of waterholes, but sufficient for them to halt and set up camp.

At the same time, William Yaldwyn had arrived at the Goulburn where his man, John Coppock was waiting for him. Coppock was to take over the lead, allowing Yaldwyn to depart with two servants to Port Phillip, where he would visit Ebden at Carlsruhe, and Mollison, old friends from Sydney. He would meet Coppock later at his new station, which he named Barfold. (Yaldwyn is remembered by the street named for him in Kyneton.)

John Coppock, a good bushman, actually considered constructing a bridge over the Goulburn to enable his stock to cross dry, after one of his men fell from his horse in a crossing attempt and drowned. The river was up to ten feet deep, quite wide, and the current was strong. Coppock

The Loddon River at Newstead. Abraham crossed here in December 1837.

eventually decided instead to swim the stock over, which he accomplished with the loss of only a handful. His drays were driven over, pulled by the bullocks.

Coppock was a considerate man and waited a full day to assist William Allen's party to cross, a gesture greatly appreciated by all concerned. The crossing went without incident, and Allen again called a halt for a further rest day for the stock. Coppock did the same.

Allen later wrote:

> 'The Goulburn River is a good stream and we were able to catch many fish there, what we called Codfish, which were very big, sometimes twenty pound or more, and there was a lot of them about. It was a real change from the boiled mutton that we mostly had to eat and got so heartily sick of. Mister Coppock was a good man to help us cross the river and we appreciated it so much as we were very tired. I broke out a good barrel of rum for the men that night and they all got drunk on it. Mister Coppock also gave us some bags of salt, flour and sugar and some tobacco, all of which we were short of, he having brought fresh supplies with him. He was very generous and treated us well.
>
>   'Captain Brown's party caught up with us and there was a great celebration. We even drank

champagne from Mister Yaldwyn's stock, and the servants were given rum, which they liked the best anyway. It was a wonderful party and I think everybody was drunk.

'In two days we were set to leave on the last leg of this exciting journey.'

Following the Major's Line, where so few had gone before, Abraham's party moved through the difficult section now known as Expedition Pass. They then crossed a small stream. This was Forest Creek, which was to become the site of the world's richest alluvial goldfield just fourteen years later. They had no inkling of the massive wealth they had bypassed.

From there they travelled through what is today the centre

The Coliban River. A dreadful massacre of native people took place not far from this tranquil spot.

of Castlemaine, crossing what became the government camp in 1851 and on to the Loddon River at present day Newstead.

Crossing the Loddon was accomplished with ease, and on December 9th, 1834, the party finally arrived at what was unmistakeably Mitchell's 'valley of the finest description', a

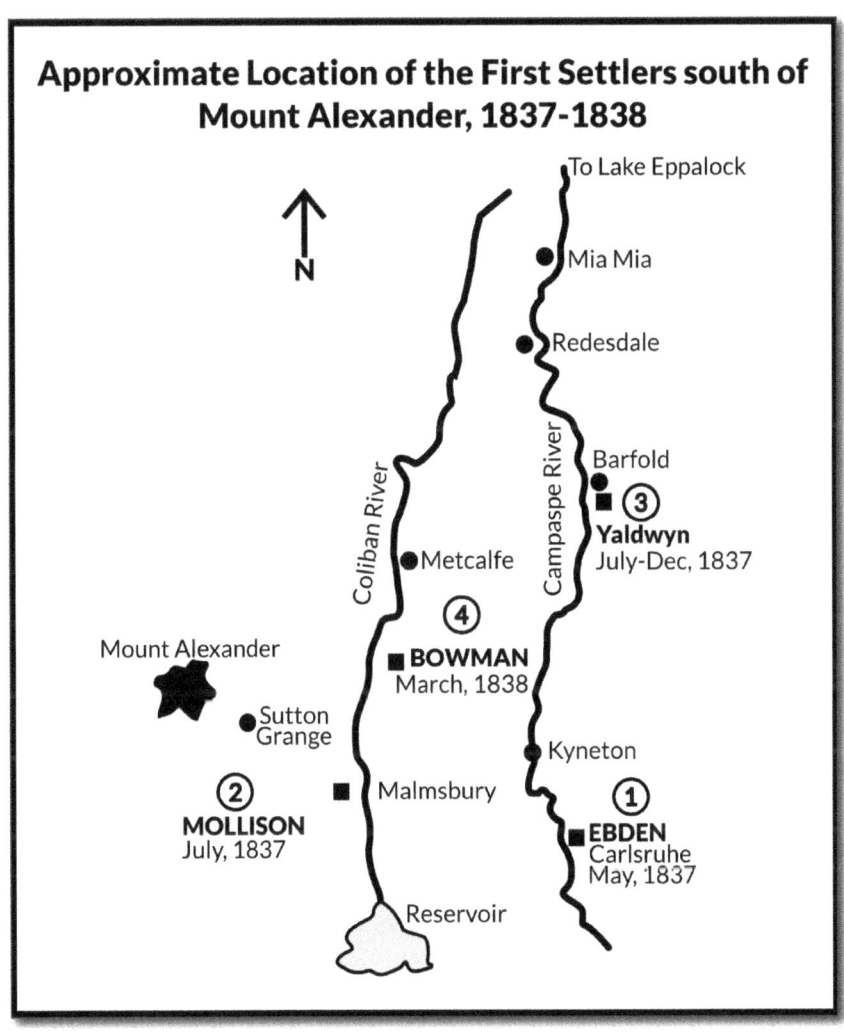

little south-east of the present Lexton township.

Abraham and his group were therefore among the first white men to pass beyond Mount Alexander – December, 1837.

Previous first settlers to the south were Charles Ebden, on the Campaspe River, at Carlsruhe in May of 1837; John Coppock, to the north of Ebden, with William Yaldwyn's stock in June, 1837; Alexander Mollison, December–January, 1837-1838 on the west bank of the Coliban River, at present day Malmsbury; and William Bowman in March, 1838, on the west bank of the Coliban, near present day Metcalfe.

The group led by Allen preceded all of these settlers, excluding Ebden and Coppock. Since Mitchell's exploration party the year before, they were the first white men to traverse what was virtually unknown country. Apprehension concerning the attitude and reaction of the Aboriginal inhabitants was a constant presence.

A note on Charles Ebden, the very first settler: Ebden had set up a couple of stations previously, unsure of where he should settle. He finally chose a spot, about 38 000 acres, on the Campaspe River south of present day Kyneton, which he named Carlsruhe, the name he had given an earlier station on the Murray River. The head station was near the long ago de-licensed Carlsruhe Hotel, which still stands. (The author had a job there in 1968, painting the iron roof red. It was then owned by German chef Benno Augustus Holtshausen)

Chapter Ten

Establishing Maiden Hills Station. Jobs allocated.
Bowerman comes to visit. Ten pounds a year rent for 50,000 acres.
Three lonely shepherds in two tents. Eight Aboriginals slaughtered.
Reprisals feared.

THE land selected by Allen for his employer lay adjacent to the scenic Pyrenees Range, so named by Thomas Mitchell because of their resemblance to the Pyrenees of Spain which Mitchell had seen during his service in the Peninsular War. It was well watered by several streams and abundant springs, among them the Doctors, Burnbank and Bet Bet creeks. These streams flowed north, eventually emptying into the Loddon River. The towering Mount Mitchell was also located on the property.

Moorakile, one of the Mammaloid Hills, viewed from Mount Kooroochieng. Photo by Glenn Braybrook.

A few kilometres south was a chain of hills named The Mammaloid Hills, also named by Mitchell, who fancied that they resembled the breasts of a reclining woman. He must have been in the bush too long!

It was exciting for the party members to be at their final destination. It had been a very hard trip and had taken a toll on them all. Although close to exhaustion, there was no let-up for the convicts. First, the hurdles had to be erected to hold the sheep, and trees felled to construct yards for the cattle, to control them until some fencing was eventually erected. Most of the twenty-three servants were engaged in this while Allen and a few select men were busy building a slab hut for the expected arrival of Henry Bowerman. He was due any day and would demand comfortable accommodation.

The men felled the trees and cut a number of them into slabs for the hut walls. The roof rafters were of saplings and

Prominent Maiden Hills area landmark, Mount Kooroochieng. Photo by Marilyn Bennet.

the covering, made from the sheets of bark, was a direct copy of the huts they had seen at Mollison's.

The furniture, although scant, had been conveyed from Yass in one of the drays. It was a reasonably comfortable hut on completion, with a stone chimney and fireplace and two wall openings to allow light to enter.

In two days, the hut and the yards were completed, and Allen ordered the men to build two shelters for themselves. Inside a week, the area resembled a small village set in the heart of a wilderness.

William Allen then allocated the various jobs. Abraham was to be the designated bootmaker, as well as sharing with John Davis and Denis Brennan, the responsibility for a mob of 3 000 sheep. Abraham was also appointed as the hutkeeper and placed in charge. The balance of the men were assigned various tasks, a majority as shepherds to be scattered throughout the station area.

Abraham's role of bootmaker was important, as boots wore out quickly in the bush where 'shank's pony' was the primary mode of travel. People regularly walked many miles and thought nothing of it. Therefore, boots had to be regularly repaired and often replaced. To begin with, each convict was issued with two pair per year. Abraham was kept busy making at least one pair each week, as well as the constant demand for repairs, with boots being delivered to him weekly.

A week after that first arrival, Henry Boucher Bowerman rode up on a fine horse, accompanied by two protective native troopers assigned to him by Captain Lonsdale. He took up residence in the hut, suggesting that the current occupier, William Allen, move out, possibly to share a hut with the convicts. Allen was not pleased and ordered the

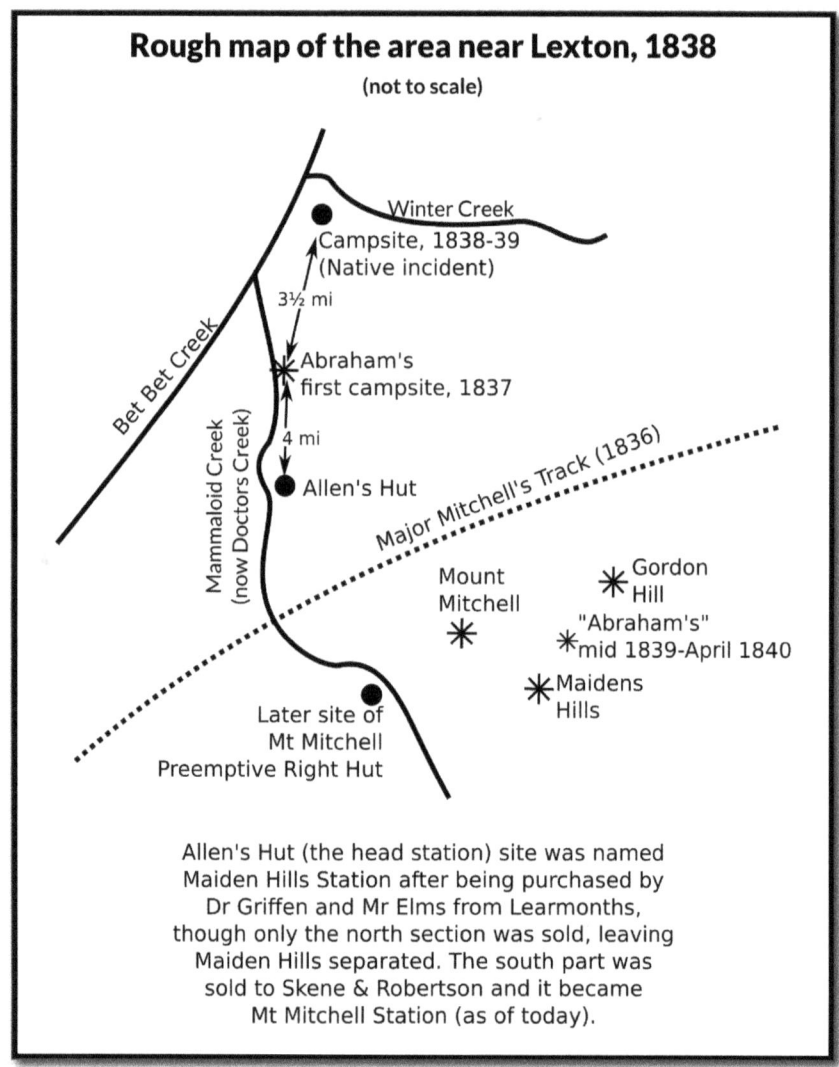

Rough sketch of the locality of the Head Station huts, first location of Bowerman's station near Lexton and site of conflict.

men to immediately construct another hut for him, which they did the same day.

The huts were built of slabs and bark and located high on the banks of Mammaloid* Creek, a delightful spot, watered by the permanent flow of the creek and a reliable spring.

Thus, Abraham Braybrook, the English convict serving a life sentence, became one of the first white men to settle in regional Victoria. Certainly his group were the first thirty to settle in the Avoca-Lexton-Ballaarat district.

For his magnificent new property, Bowerman would pay a trifling ten pounds a year rent, the ruling rate for the 'pure merinos' and other gentlemen. Bowerman stayed on until late October, putting the place in order to his liking. There was relief (not the least for William Allen, who got his comfortable hut back) when Bowerman returned by ship to Sydney to be home with his family for Christmas. The master returned again briefly during the first month of 1839, checking on his various speculative land investments in Port Phillip at the same time. He went home to Sydney but it wasn't long before he was compelled to return to Port Phillip (by now named Melbourne, having been given that name by Governor Bourke on his visit there in March 1837).

At the time of Abraham's arrival at Maiden Hills, Melbourne was nothing more than a miserable-looking port town populated by about 600 people, not counting the 130 convicts engaged in road building and building of

---

* *Now Doctors Creek, named after Doctor John Griffen who later occupied the run.*

government offices and homes. The village's existence was justified to serve the needs of the small number of squatters, such as Fawkner and Batman. There were perhaps fifty scattered houses, mostly rickety huts of one or two rooms.

Along the Yarra River, several rough wharf sheds held imported goods guarded by savage dogs. On the higher ground on what was to become Collins Street, a straggle of down at heel shops mixed with several low-grade buildings that served as hotels. On Eastern Hill were three houses spread over a wide area.

The Police Magistrate's house was described by a contemporary as 'no more than a wooden box' set alongside three military huts described as 'hovels'. The police office had walls only five feet high, made of rammed earth, topped

The Waubra wind farm in 2019. Part of Major Mitchell's "Valley of the Finest Description". ABC News.

by a sod roof spread over bush saplings. Whenever it served as a court-house, a packing case was inverted as the bench, and empty kegs served as seats. Police Magistrate Lonsdale was the most senior government official in Melbourne until he was superseded, in 1839, by an official of higher rank, Superintendent Charles Joseph Latrobe (later Governor). The entire population of the Port Phillip district, the present-day state of Victoria, was around 1 500, seventy percent of which was male.

In early 1838, Abraham, John Davis and fourteen-year-old Denis Brennan were sent out to the north of the run with their lot of sheep. Abraham was in charge and responsible overall.

Initially they established a camp on the banks of the Mammaloid Creek, about four miles from the head station, and they stayed there until the new year of 1839. The immediate area had become grazed out and Allen ordered them to move further north where he had selected a suitable site for them.

It was a most picturesque spot, on a bank overlooking two creeks, one of them a delightful stream known today as Doctors Creek. The other was a minor winter creek called xxxx* by the natives, a name it retains to this day. The area was surrounded by steep embankments and grassy hills.

Other than along the creeks, few trees grew; a legacy of the destruction of the forest by early volcanic eruptions. To

---

*   *The name is not given, as the precise location will not be generally revealed so as to preserve the site.*

the south, beyond a steep rise extending over half a mile, stretched a wide and fertile plain which ran almost to the head station, seven miles away.

* * *

This was a devastatingly lonely and isolated spot, as remote as it was beautiful. Even today, it is so remote as to be visited by the landowner maybe just once every two or three years.

The trio set up camp on a high southern bank at the intersection of the two creeks, below a huge and spreading red gum tree. The site provided a clear view for 360 degrees, important for observing the sheep and for keeping a constant eye out for Aborigines.

The camp consisted of two sturdy canvas tents to serve as portable huts, each twelve by nine feet (4 by 3 metres), set about seventy feet (twenty metres) apart. The furniture was rough and sparse – a bed made from bark spread over thick logs, a rough, bush-made table and a chair. At the end of one hut, a rough stone fireplace was constructed, as this was likely to be a more permanent camp. This hut served as a sort of living room for the three and as an occasional bedroom for Abraham. It also served as his bootmaking workshop. As the hutkeeper in charge of the unit, his nights were usually spent in the watch-box, guarding the sheep. His days were spent making boots.

Cooking was done outdoors on an open campfire, unless the weather was too bad, which it sometimes was in winter. Davis occupied the second tent with young Brennan.

Ancient river red gums, many well over two hundred years old, lined the two creeks, much the same as they still do in some parts today. Even in the driest summers, Doctors Creek retains abundant, delightful waterholes, which in the pioneering days, probably swarmed with native fish, in all ways a great attraction to wildlife and man. Birds of a vast array still sing where platypus once swam and kangaroos and wallabies flourish. It was the type of spot that was extremely important to Aborigines, and occupancy by white intruders was bound to cause resentment.

There was much fear abroad at the time, as there had been a number of serious clashes between squatters and the natives. A number of shepherds, stuck as they were in lonely outposts, had been slain or injured by the Blacks. A very serious outrage took place in August of 1838 following a sheep-stealing incident on Bowman's station, a day's ride away from Abraham's. This property adjoined William Yaldwyn's to the west.

A shepherd was speared to death and his body disembowelled. Then some sheep were stolen and Yaldwyn's overseer, John Coppock, got up a group to hunt down the offenders. This resulted in the mindless slaughter of a reported eight Aboriginals, but probably more, as a number were badly wounded. It is believed that this grisly event took place at what is now Waterloo Flat.

The natives had never seen a gun fired and had no idea what the weapon could do. It was easy pickings for men with guns, some are said to have regarded the hunting down of natives as a bizarre form of sport. Sadly, it appears that in some instances, it was true.

The fear of attack by natives was with all men in these outposts. Abraham, Davis and Brennan would certainly have been among them and, if placed in their isolated position, it would be easy for us to understand their fear.

Chapter Eleven

*Settling into a new camp. Shepherd's rations. Solitude.
Sheep and shoes. First encounter with natives. Haircuts and meat.
Female company? Allen warns natives off.*

By the new year of 1839, Abraham, John Davis and young Denis Brennan had settled well into the life of being shepherds in this lonely place.

Davis was serving only seven years and hoped to go home one day, having come out on the *Lady Nugent* in 1835. Young Brennan was only fourteen, also serving seven years, and had come out on the *Waterloo* in 1836. Abraham had been in the colony the longest and entertained no hope of ever going home. His sentence forbade him ever returning to Great Britain.

It is difficult for those who live in the twenty-first century to comprehend the isolation and loneliness of these shepherds' lives. Even now the district is sparsely occupied. The home station hut, occupied by William Allen, was seven miles from Abraham's camp and was itself exceedingly isolated from civilisation. The shepherds had no horse, so all travel was on foot. If it became necessary to contact Allen, young Brennan was called on to walk to the head station.

Once each week, a drayman delivered supplies and provisions, usually flour, tea, sugar, salt and mutton. Potatoes were usually included and, in season, some other form of vegetables that were now being grown at the head station; this to prevent scurvy. It was quite a monotonous diet, but was relieved by Davis's ability to make acceptable johnnycakes in the camp oven or fried in mutton fat. Catfish and other native fish were also plentiful and easily caught. Wild ducks frequented the waterholes and were often trapped in devices fashioned by the men, so it was a good diet by the standards of the time.

Although shepherds worked among sheep, they were generally forbidden to slaughter any for food. Under the rules, they were held accountable for the numbers in their care and any losses had to be proven. Overseer Allen, however, closed his eyes to a limited violation of the rule by

Site of controversial slayings. Alan (r) and Ian Braybrook.

Abraham and occasionally sheep were slaughtered, but strictly as required.

Generally, the shepherds' food and clothing were rationed, in line with the government regulations. Tobacco was included in fairly generous quantities, and rum was issued at a quart a man each week, at the discretion of the overseer. Tea was rationed to a mere one ounce per man per week, enough for only a couple of pots of the weakest brew. The tea leaves were then dried for re-use.

This campsite on the banks of Doctors Creek was exceptionally isolated, and ever present was their deeply ingrained fear of Aboriginal attack and murder. Any present-day visitor to the site will testify to the solitude that still prevails there – apart from the usual sounds of nature, there is total silence, broken perhaps by the drone of a high-flying aircraft as it heads northward towards Darwin.

Apart from themselves, the shepherds' only company were the two sheepdogs, invaluable in controlling and herding the mob, particularly at night. The days of these men who tended the sheep were filled in caring for the flock, checking and removing any blowfly strike, crutching to remove dags and keeping the sheep from straying beyond specific areas. Abraham spent much daylight time in his tent making boots and shoes.

At night, the mob was herded together into enclosures fabricated from portable bush-timber hurdles, in a different area every few nights to prevent foot rot developing from churned, damp soil. In addition, at shearing time it was the shepherds' job to help wash the sheep in the creek to partly cleanse the fleece, thus adding considerable value to the clip.

Abraham's additional job of making boots for the convicts and free men held by Bowerman was essential in those times when boots wore out quickly, as men went everywhere on foot. The leather and other materials were sent out with the regular weekly supplies as required. Abraham was an important man to the operation of the station, and his skills and general competence were highly valued by William Allen.

Life went on in its humdrum way until one pleasant March morning in 1839. Abraham was startled to observe in the distance a group of perhaps thirty naked Aboriginals, men, women and children. Abraham had come across Aborigines before, but a long way in the distance. Although they appeared friendly enough, he and his companions were afraid of them, the talk of William Allen in their minds.

The weather had remained hot into the early autumn that year, and the Aboriginals rarely wore coverings unless cold. Undoubtedly the sight of several naked, attractive young women proved a thought-provoking temptation to the youthful shepherds. The group stood beneath trees about 300 metres along the far bank of the small winter creek, where a great deal of gesturing and loud talking was taking place. Obviously the natives were quite disturbed at the view that met their eyes, a sight probably totally unexpected and extremely distressing. It was most likely the custom of this nomadic clan, to return to the idyllic site each autumn to set up a camp. Here they would take advantage of the abundance of fish and game available during the approaching winter period. The hills around also grew large quantities of murnong*, a plant whose root the women collected and roasted in their ovens; part of their staple diet and vital to survival.

To have property that had been theirs for generations occupied by interloping white men would have been a shocking surprise. By a series of gestures, words and signals, Abraham and John managed to gain some trust from the natives and they cautiously approached, spears at the ready. Thinking quickly, Abraham made a decision to offer the people food and seized a side of mutton that hung from a low branch outside his tent. He extended the meat toward them. The offer proved to be too much to resist and two of the men approached, taking the proffered meat, accompanied by considerable babble in their own language, while moving quickly away.

Over the ensuing days the natives returned regularly, to be rewarded by further gifts of meat and small quantities of flour. Soon the Aboriginals became most friendly and trustful, possibly offering the shepherds use of their women in return for the food.

We do not speculate on this matter, except to say that, fit, testosterone-fuelled young men, who had no contact whatsoever with females of any age, colour or demeanour,

---

* *The root of the daisy-like plant abundant in the area at the time; now uncommon due to sheep grazing.*

may have been sorely tempted by the young women on offer.

Sexual engagement with native women was a perennial and widespread practice with both master and servant. Assistant Protector Sievwright actually arrested and charged two men in September 1839. They each received fifty lashes of the 'cat', but the practice continued unabated. There is an old and appropriate saying: 'A standing member has no conscience.'

So trusting became the relationship that the natives, observing Davis cutting Abraham's hair, accepted the offer to have their hair cut. The entire clan gathered to watch as Davis carried out the job on each of them, an operation that caused great mirth, a task spread over two days.

During this time, the requests for fresh mutton became more and more demanding, in fact downright hostile, as refusal followed refusal. Abraham tried in vain to explain that he could not slaughter sheep in volume for fear of punishment from Allen. The men were displeased and let Abraham know their feelings by a series of signals and utterances, but they were not belligerent or threatening.

William Allen had ordered that any sighting or approach of Aboriginals must be reported to him, so eventually, the boy, Brennan, was despatched on foot to the head station. Allen was furious when told of the natives' presence and immediately rode to locate them. When he came upon them, he demonstrated clearly by word, gesture and discharge of his gun into the air, that they were not welcome and must stay away from the shepherds and the camp.

Allen returned to the shepherds and told them sharply that if the Aboriginals made any further visits, he must be summoned immediately, and that he would 'deal with them'. His dislike for Aboriginals was patently obvious. He particularly hated the fraternisation of white men with native women who, squatters claimed, gave men diseases that prevented them from working. He would not tolerate this behaviour and his prisoner workers knew this well.

Site of the controversial encounter with Aborigines.

Chapter Twelve

Melbourne, 1839. Captain William Lonsdale.
George Augustus Robinson, Protector of Aborigines.
Charles Sievwright. The ride to Maiden Hills.
Sievwright meets Allen.

MELBOURNE is 150 miles from Maiden Hills station, several days hard ride on horseback, but a journey often undertaken by men such as William Allen who sought a taste of civilised life. In April 1839, the bayside settlement had grown into a bustling village, with accompanying facilities, primitive roads, buildings, streets and filth. Six hundred people lived there and the town had developed steadily. Land values had increased at an astonishing rate as investors saw a bright future for the place. The buildings were quite small, even the business buildings; the Bank of Australasia for example, was in a four-room building, which included the residence of the manager and staff.

The town was bounded by Lonsdale, Flinders, Swanston and William Streets. The new suburb of Collingwood (named Newtown in 1839) was developing and accommodated about a dozen houses.

The infrastructure had not by any means kept pace and there was much room for improvement. (It is apparently still that way in the 21st century!)

When it rained, the streets became a sea of foul sludge,

Collins Street, Melbourne, 1839. Watercolour by W. Knight via Wikipedia.

and shoppers were forced to wade through ankle deep muck. Elizabeth Street, formerly a winter creek, became a raging torrent when heavy rains fell, and people were in fear of drowning. Gullies over two metres deep and fifteen metres wide were excavated by the rains.

Most of the timber had been cleared from the surveyed streets but many huge, immovable stumps remained, a hazard for horse and carriage, especially at night. Street lighting was virtually non-existent, although a man was contracted to light the four oil burners on Collins Street each night. More often than not, they were extinguished by blasts of wind.

After rain, horses and horsedrawn vehicles ploughed their way through the mud, further stirring the mess into a stinking sludge.

Sanitation in the town was primitive, with human waste and a variety of rubbish buried in backyard holes or even dumped on the surface. The muck ultimately seeped into the mud and made its way into the Yarra Yarra. Mounds of disgusting waste product from abattoir and tannery rotted in the yards and paddocks, and a constant stench pervaded the air. It was not the most desirable place to live!

Nevertheless, the place was an attraction to young men from wealthy families of the Old Country, particularly Scotland, who saw great potential for profit in the colony. They brought with them a great deal of money and were able to take up huge areas of land for practically nought, laying the foundations for many a fortune, especially in the Western District.

The man in charge of the settlement, was 36-year-old ex-Army Captain, William Lonsdale, Police Magistrate, appointed to the position by Governor Bourke two years before. His office was a tiny room in the police office set on a rise above Flinders Street. Next door was the police lockup.

Lonsdale resided in a modest cottage on the eastern hill, and not far from his cottage was the home and offices of George Augustus Robinson, Chief Protector of Aborigines. His offices were equally small; two rooms each thirteen by seven feet (about 4 by 2 metres). His two-room brick cottage was next door.

George Augustus Robinson, Chief Protector of Aborigines, Port Phillip District. Detail from painting by Benjamin Duterrau (1767–1851) Tasmania Museum and Art Gallery.

Here, a brief word about Robinson: George Augustus Robinson was a Hobart carpenter, a devout Christian, who is famed for his four-year-long walk around the perimeter of Tasmania.

Setting off from Hobart in the company of four Aboriginal guides in February, 1830 his determined intention was to 'Christianise' any native inhabitants he encountered and demonstrate that not all white people were bad news. Men who were experienced said he was a fool at best and what he proposed was impossible; the country was too wild and impenetrable.

But conquer this mountainous, cold, wet land of thick forest he did, finally arriving at Cape Grim on the far north-west coast in June, 1830. Along the way, the scattering of natives he encountered ran off when they saw him, so he achieved little of his purpose.

He was greeted similarly as he covered the north coast and headed east. In the latter region the Aborigines had been treated so badly by white men, with countless numbers allegedly murdered, they fled on seeing his approach. Therefore he saw very few, let alone was he able to Christianise them.

Robinson was finally able to convince the remnants of the Big River tribe to move to near Hobart.

Eventually, he moved to protect and preserve as many natives as he could locate to Flinders Island. Here he was placed in charge by the Governor. When he left the island to take up his appointment as Chief Protector of Aborigines in Port Phillip, only eighty remained alive; as well, there was an increasing number of deaths – probably from white man's diseases

In his new job, Robinson was to receive a huge salary (for the time) of five hundred pounds a year, the highest paid government employee by far. George Augustus Robinson's place in the history of our nation is assured.

One April day, Robinson was seated at his desk composing a letter to one of his assistants, 35-year-old Charles Wightman Sievwright J.P. Just as modern day people use email to contact work colleagues, so were letters the common form of inter-department contact in 1839.

Robinson wrote to Sievwright in a clear, bold hand and in a language we find quaint today:

> Sir.
> Understanding a rumour to be in circulation that two Aboriginal Natives have been shot on the Geelong Road at a station belonging to a Mr Allen. I have therefore to request that you are to make a full investigation into this affair and report the result of your inquiry to this office.
> 'I should scarcely have thought it necessary to have directed this inquiry since I hardly believe that the lives of two fellow creatures should have been thus destroyed unless some justifiable cause has warranted the transaction.

Robinson added a postscript stating that he now had information that a person connected with the shooting was actually in town, and, having reported to Captain Lonsdale, had felt no need to do more. He urged Sievwright to act swiftly.

> 'Blacks are equally protected under law with whites and can no longer be destroyed with impunity.'

The person in town that Robinson referred to was William Allen, overseer of Bowerman's Maiden Hills Station. He was in Melbourne primarily to visit his brother; reporting the incident involving the Blacks was secondary and unimportant to him. He informed Lonsdale that two natives had been shot by two assigned servants in fear of their lives as they had been attacked in a raid to steal blankets and flour.

His duty done, he commenced to have a good time before returning to Maiden Hills next morning.

By the time Sievwright received his order from Robinson, William Allen was miles away, probably halfway home. There was nothing for Sievwright to do but follow.

From the beginning, Sievwright was sceptical of what he thought was a 'feeble report' allowed to lie dormant, and he considered that it was only by chance that it had come to the notice of Robinson. Sievwright suspected that Allen had a greater role in the shootings than he had let on.

His first task was to find a suitable mount and, hopefully, a mounted trooper to accompany him on the long ride. Robinson advised Sievwright that he should call for the company and assistance of Mr Edward Parker, Assistant Protector in the Loddon Region (now Franklinford, below Mount Franklin).

Sievwright ignored this request, as, only days before, he had experienced a serious altercation with Parker, who alleged that Sievwright had been having an affair with his wife!

He advised Robinson of his need for a good horse, but his chief was unable to locate one. Sievwright was eventually able to obtain a mount on loan from the police service.

Life in the Bush: The Squatter's First Home by A.D. Lang. Coloured lithograph in the Latrobe Collection, State Library of Victoria.

He was grudgingly assigned a Black trooper to assist, in case any arrests were necessary. On April 3rd, 1839, he set off toward what was known as the Julien Range*, itself an epic journey.

The track to the Pyrenees district ran from Geelong and was not often travelled. It was used by the occasional rider such as William Allen and very few others and was almost indiscernible in parts. On leaving Geelong, Sievwright took the direction toward Buninyong and the Warrang-geip Mountains (Mount Warrenheip), navigating mostly by compass, but when he and his companion were well short of that landmark, they became lost in fog and thick bush. They

---

* *Despite extensive enquiry, the precise location of the Jullian Range is unknown. It was the last range of hills crossed by Hume and Hovell before arriving at Port Phillip. They are possibly the hills around Kinglake and Beveridge.*

were forced to backtrack a full day until by chance they came upon a group of local natives who agreed to conduct them through the district to Mount Warrenheip. This cost Sievwright two days, and he did not locate the Maiden Hills station until April 8th.

He wrote in his journal that he 'located the house station of Bowerman 160 miles from Melbourne. It is a most beautiful place half way between the Julien Range and the Grampians.'

Allen was in residence in the comfortable hut built for Bowerman, located in an elbow of Mammaloid Creek*. According to Sievwright, it was 'contiguous to the track of Major Mitchell'.

Allen did not welcome the visit of an Aboriginal Protector, and he had not realised that such an organization existed. He was certainly surprised by the visit.

Sievwright was unimpressed by the sight of a skull nailed above the door of the hut. He was certain it was the skull of an Aboriginal, but Allen said that it was a skull he found on a ride over the plains, and he intended to hand it to a doctor friend for study in due course. Sievwright did not hide his scepticism and questioned Allen further. Allen admitted that the skull was displayed as a deterrent to native visitors.

---

* *Now Doctor's Creek named after Dr Griffen who, with Mr Elms, later occupied the hut for a short time. They purchased some of the Maiden Hills property from the Learmonth brothers, who had obtained it from Henry Bowerman. In 1847, the site became part of Woodstock Station. A contemporary painting by Mister Lang, is believed to be the hut in question. The man seated at the fireplace is believed to be Dr Griffen*

The Protector was invited into the hut for a welcome meal and a good night's sleep. The native trooper was lodged in a tent.

Sievwright began his close questioning of Allen, asking why he had not reported the incident to Chief Protector Robinson, as instructed by Lonsdale. Allen replied that he thought he had done enough.

Sievwright, who was a Justice of the Peace, then took a signed deposition from Allen. The overseer stated that Dennis Brennan had come to him one day about a month earlier and told him that natives were visiting the camp, even on that very day they were there. The Blacks had indicated that they would bring their women with them the next day. This undoubtedly alarmed Allen in his belief that the native women gave shepherds syphilis and gonorrhoea and thus prevented them from doing their jobs.

His orders were that the shepherds must report any presence of natives to him, 'that I may be prepared for them'. Allen continued that he rode to the camp next morning, and Abraham told him that the natives had been seen early, about 200 yards away. Abraham said that they were on good terms and were not afraid of the natives. 'I then rode in the direction the men indicated that the Aboriginals had gone and located the native women four miles off. I observed the men about three miles distant running in the opposite direction.' Allen then returned to the camp and again warned the men not to allow the natives to come near them, as 'I know their intention'.

At that time, Abraham told Allen that if the natives came in small numbers they would welcome them, as they wanted to remain on good terms.

According to his statement, Allen had been back at his hut only an hour when young Brennan ran up with the story of the shootings and the attack on the two shepherds.

Allen said that he believed that the natives were trying to keep Davis in his tent while the others secured what they came for. At the same time, he believed that Abraham was attacked in his tent, and, as he forced his way past his would-be captors, one of the native women was thrust upon him and they 'gave him to understand that the girl was at his disposal'.

Abraham had rushed from the tent with two fowling pieces, but the natives pinioned his arms, although he held onto the guns, and marched him to Davis's tent. Inside he was hit on the head by a waddy and he called upon Davis to fire. Davis did so, and one ball struck the Aboriginal in the chest, upon which he seized Abraham's arm in his teeth. Davis then shot the man in the breast and he fell dead. The shepherds then ran outside and fired at another of the assailants, who were throwing waddies, striking the native in the groin and the upper arm.

On arrival at the scene, Allen said that he ordered the bodies to be burnt, as he had no digging implements and felt it was 'more congenial to the custom of the natives'.

He further stated on oath that he had never ordered his men to shoot Aboriginals, 'unless they commenced hostilities in the first instance'.

Allen undertook a bond of one hundred pounds to ensure that he appeared as a witness if required.

Sievwright was sceptical of the evidence of Allen and noted this in his journal:

> 'I observed discrepancies in evidence. Allen was agitated – it appeared that the shepherds had been on good terms with the natives before and prior to Allen's visit to the camp where he had gone, in his own words, that he might be ready for them as he knew what they came for.'

Sievwright also noted that it was an accepted fact that Aboriginals never took the women with them when they were going to attack.

> 'These convince me that the visit of Allen was the cause of alarm in Davis and Braybrook and they were stimulated, if not ordered to act as they had done. Allen became very agitated and confused, especially when he stated that he ordered that the bodies should be burnt.'

Sievwright was unimpressed with Allen and concluded: 'There was much more to be learned than what he (Allen) had stated'. He added, 'I much fear that further acts of atrocity and bloodshed will be perpetrated from the spirit of animosity that seems to pervade.'

The next morning, Sievwright, accompanied by the trooper, rode the seven miles north-west to Abraham's camp to continue his investigation. A short distance off he came upon a large red gum tree engraved with the names of Thomas Mitchell and his party and dated 1836, and he made special note of this in his journal.

He wrote again:

> 'I am convinced that the visit of Allen was the cause of unnecessary alarm in Braybrook and Davis and they were stimulated, if not ordered by him, to act as they had done.'

Chapter Thirteen

Sievwright at the camp. The killings site.
Depositions from all involved. Arrests and murder charges.
Sievwright is sceptical of Allen. Off to Melbourne.

SIEVWRIGHT could not help but be impressed by the beautiful and productive land that he saw as he rode. Early autumn rains had turned the countryside a splendid green. The view from the extensive flat plateau that led to the lengthy slope to the shepherds' campsite was enchanting. To the east was a bank of eucalypts, the edge of a forest that extends deep toward what is now Talbot. There were few trees in the area that he traversed; instead, the ground was heavily strewn with volcanic rocks, many of them huge. The rock cover became much thicker and made it difficult for the horses to pick a path through the long grass as the two men rode down the slope to approach the camp by the creeks.

At the camp, the three shepherds, astonished to be receiving visitors, extended a warm welcome to them. Their usual visitors were the natives, the drayman with the weekly provisions and, occasionally, William Allen.

Assistant Protector Sievwright wasted little time on small talk, but happily accepted a cup of tea. Abraham and his companions were surprised at the reason for the visit and were quite unprepared for any questioning about the slaying of the Blacks.

As hutkeeper, Abraham was the spokesman for the trio and was quite open about the incident, although nervous. He conducted Sievwright to a blackened spot beside a fallen gum tree some 200 metres from the tents, on the southern bank of the Caralulup Creek. At this time of year the creek was dry. Sievwright was told that this was the spot where the men burned the dead bodies of the two Aboriginals that they had shot. They made no attempt to conceal the fact that they had shot the natives or that they had destroyed the bodies.

'It took two full days to burn them,' Abraham said. He went on to say that it had taken a lot of their supply of wood, and they had burnt the dead on the orders of Mr Allen. The men appeared to feel little guilt over their actions, apparently satisfied that the slayings were justified and that the burnings were in order. Sievwright later wrote that he felt that both incidents were at the order or instruction of their master, and they had no say in the matters.

The Protector of Aborigines sifted through the funeral pyre ashes in the hope that he would find some evidence of the crime. His only reward was a tiny fragment of bone, a near dust portion of the skull of one victim, which he placed carefully in his saddlebag for transport to Melbourne.

Sievwright was suspicious, particularly of Allen. He felt that his story did not ring true. Why did he order the burning of the bodies? Was it intended to cover up – to destroy any evidence of a crime? There was little or no evidential material and no chance of a post-mortem examination of the dead.

He proceeded to question Davis and Abraham who, Allen had told him, had shot the two men. He conducted the questioning separately, to allow for comparison of the stories, knowing that the two were totally unprepared and had no chance to collaborate.

Their replies left Sievwright in no doubt that a crime had occurred, and he recorded the three shepherds' statements on paper, a written deposition to present to a later court. He formally charged Abraham and Davis with murder, and both men did not hesitate to plead guilty. He advised them that they would be committed for trial on a charge of murder, and that he would advise the Attorney General in Sydney where the trial must be held. He said that he intended to write down their answers to further questions and that they would be required to sign the papers to confirm their accuracy. How men who could not read or write could be expected to confirm the written word is not explained.

Abraham stated that he was indeed guilty of shooting a Black. Sievwright wrote in his own sort of shorthand as Abraham spoke, urging him to speak slowly.

> 'I was in me tent workin' when blackfellers came to the door. I looked past 'em and saw others carrying orf me blankets from me watch box. If I lost those Mr Allen would really punish me 'ard. I called out to John for 'elp an' at the same time I 'eard 'im call for 'elp. I ran past the blacks at me door, carryin' with me my two fowlin'

pieces, all primed up with powder an' shot. At John's tent a blackfeller 'it me on the 'ead with a bloody waddy. It didn't 'urt much but I was scared. I called to John to fire and 'e shot a round. The black was 'it but still upon me and 'e bit me and John fired again into the man's chest and the black fell. I grabbed a fowlin' piece and ran outta the tent an' there was more blacks. I fired into one man's chest and John came out and fired a shot to finish 'im. The natives then ran orf, takin' me blankets and two pairs of the trousers of John and Denis with 'em.

'Me orders from Mister Allen was to protect ourselves an' the sheep and our stuff. Before this the natives was always friendly like, an' did what we told 'em and we 'ad no quarrel with 'em.'

Abraham signed his deposition with an X and it was witnessed by P. Keitty (presumably the trooper).

John Davis pleaded guilty to shooting two Blacks, and he told a similar story. He said that he saw a group of natives at Abraham's tent and heard him call out for help as they were taking things from his watch-box. A native had meanwhile placed himself at the doorway of Davis' tent. He moved to help Abraham, but the native pushed him back inside. He called to Abraham for help, and when his mate came into the tent, the native struck him on the head with a waddy.

'The black then pinioned Abraham's arms, so I took my piece and shot him in the belly. He did not fall so I took my other piece and shot him in the breast. He then fell and Abraham went outside. I heard the sound of a shot from his piece and I went out in time to see the native trying to hit Abraham with a waddy. I shot him in the arm. I think the first shot of Abraham's had hit him in the belly. The others ran away and we could have shot more but did not.

'My orders from Mr Allen were to protect ourselves and the property. The bodies were burned the next day. A few days before, the natives had come up and I had cut the hair of several of them and also a second day.'

Davis could write his name and signed the deposition.

Denis Brennan signed a brief statement in which he declared that he was not present when the shooting occurred, but heard the shots. On returning to the camp, he saw two dead Blacks on the ground, and Abraham had told him to run and fetch Mister Allen, which he did. He said that Allen 'immediately came down'.

His work at the camp finished, Sievwright returned to the head station to take a deposition from Allen's assistant, James Oliver.

Oliver stated that he accompanied Allen to the site and that Braybrook had told him that the natives had wished him to 'leave one of their women', which made him suspicious. He said that Allen had ordered him to send a man with a spade next morning to bury the dead, but had learned later that the bodies had been burned, contrary to his order from Allen.

Sievwright then obtained a pledge of a one hundred pound bond from Allen to ensure that he appeared in court as a witness when called to the trial. His work at Maiden Hills completed, Sievwright and his trooper, on horseback, led their captives on the long trek to Melbourne. We trust that Abraham made good-wearing and comfortable boots, as he and John Davis had to walk.

Chapter Fourteen

The long walk to Melbourne. The Stockade.
LaTrobe and Lonsdale informed. The hierarchy alarmed.
The public prosecutor intervenes.
The trial and the jurymen. Charges altered. Overseer Allen appears.
Controversy. A town divided. The verdict.

It was a long way to Melbourne in 1839, a lonely journey, with the constant concern that the natives may be hostile, although the experience of Sievwright on the trip north had been undisturbed. The track was easier to follow on the return journey, as Sievwright had ensured that the trail was clearly blazed, following his experience at Buninyong.

Walking was the common mode of movement for the proletariat in those days, and it would not have been seen as remarkable to walk 150 miles. Even for Sievwright and the native trooper, it was a tiring and arduous journey, mounted as they were. For Abraham and Davis it must have been quite exhausting walking in irons. On their minds would have been the real prospect of facing the hangman, and, probably, the thought of attempting escape entered their minds. Perhaps better to be shot running away than to hang. However, the trip proved to be uneventful.

The quartet arrived in Melbourne late on April 16th, 1839. The two prisoners were confined to the Stockade to await trial. This was probably on the site of the soon to be constructed Old Melbourne Gaol which is a tourist attraction in the present day, most famed as the place where Ned Kelly was hanged.

As the name suggests, the Stockade was an area of about 200 feet square in all (about 60m×60m), entirely surrounded by high slab walls. Accommodation was several rough huts in which prisoners were locked from dark to daylight. The rest of the time was spent at work. The huts were primitive timber structures that provided the bare minimum of protection from the elements and a comfort area of nil. They were guarded by a small contingent of troopers.

The next day, Charles Sievwright went to his office early to write a report to his superior, George Robinson, in which he detailed his experiences at Maiden Hills and that he was charging the men with murder.

His decision to charge two white men with the murder of two Aboriginals caused a furore among residents of Melbourne and the settlers of the Port Phillip district. There was generally little or no sympathy for the native population, and *The Port Phillip Gazette*, in particular, was loud in condemnation of the decision.

Chief Protector George Robinson immediately wrote to Governor Latrobe outlining details of the case against Abraham Braybrook and his mate John Davis. He also informed Captain Lonsdale of the intention to charge the two men with murder.

Meanwhile, the wheels within the hierarchy of the colony began to turn, and, oddly enough, were to turn in favour of two worthless, convict shepherds! Not because of any human feeling toward these scoundrels, but fear of the potential consequences for all of the squattocracy and gentry, some of whom, it was sometimes said, rather enjoyed hunting down Aboriginals. Some also said that if it was not actually enjoyed, it was regarded as essential destruction of vermin, equal to eliminating pests, diseases and weeds.

Pain lingered strongly from the previous December when, in the settled areas beyond Sydney, seven men were found guilty of slaying Aboriginals and were hanged.

* * *

I digress here, as the Myall Creek massacre story is relevant and worth telling.

Late in 1838, squatter John Fleming led a gang of men, eleven of whom were assigned servants, in what is now known as the Myall Creek massacre. Fleming had no reason whatsoever to harm the Aborigines. This murderous day represents one of the most shameful events in our history. It was a planned, deliberate attack on the Wirrayaraang people who were camped on Myall Creek station. This small clan was peaceful and friends to many white people, even speaking a little English. The men worked on surrounding stations.

When the gang arrived at the camp the men were absent at their jobs. The gang seized the twenty-eight women, children and old men, tying their hands behind their backs.

There followed a horrific scene as the people were roughly beheaded with swords. Only one was spared, a young woman who was gang-raped many times. There are reports that the men away at work were also found and they too were slaughtered, but this is not on record.

Other station owners reported the atrocity, and the assigned servants were arrested and put on trial, their defence costs met by squatters headed by one Henry Dagnar. The jury found them not guilty.

The Attorney General then had another try, and he had the eleven put on trial for the murder of one native boy named Charley. Seven of them were found guilty and were hung. The remaining four were released when a crucial witness, an Aboriginal boy named Davey, who was to testify on their alleged role in the murders, could not be located. The charges were therefore dropped. It is claimed that Dagnar had Davey killed.

Dagnar later became a magistrate and politician. Oddly enough, his biographers usually make no reference to Myall Creek.

Amazingly, John Fleming, the squatter who led the group, was never charged.

★ ★ ★

The hanging of seven white men caused outrage among the squattocracy, pure merinos and the exclusives of Sydney Town. The thought that white men could be despatched for removing vermin was unthinkable, and there was serious unrest and anger, with animated discussions in clubs and dining rooms. There was an undercurrent of impending revolt against Governor Gipps. The hanging of more white men in Melbourne, so soon on the heels of this outrageous affair, had to be avoided. It was this that certainly saved Abraham Braybrook and John Davis from the long walk to the gallows.

The Port Phillip Gazette was extremely vocal in its populist protest against the prospect of hanging more white men, but their commentary was quite restrained when compared to *The Sydney Herald*, which ran a number of leading articles. It warned that colonists would,

> '... take the administration of justice into their own hands if Gipps and his overpaid Whiggish lawyers dared to punish another white man for alleged outrages against blacks, till all those blacks who have murdered whites shall be tried and executed.'

The Port Phillip Patriot, always a supporter of Aborigines and Robinson's Protectorate, was scathing of the *Herald's* radical views, describing the items as base, destructive, mean and cowardly. The editor of the *Patriot* wrote that the *Herald* made a great fuss about murder of white men, but showed no concern for Blacks who were 'very seldom the aggressors'. The *Gazette* editorials were in direct contrast, describing the Blacks as 'one degree above the brute creation' and 'restless, treacherous and vindictive'.

There was much anger and outrage throughout the colony.

The case of Abraham Braybrook and John Davis had caused a sensation.

A way round the situation had to be found, and soon. Attorney General, John Plunkett, came up with a sop. On May 25th, 1839, Plunkett wrote to Lonsdale that he felt that Assistant Protector Sievwright may have been a little carried away in his enthusiasm to commit the men for trial.

> 'I am of the opinion that there is not sufficient evidence to warrant me, in the exercise of my more extensive discretion, in putting them on trial for murder. I decline to prosecute them for murder.'

He added that he believed that Allen was equally guilty being 'much to blame for the burning of the bodies'. He stated that the evidence indicated to him that the slayings were in self-defence and that there was no evidence to contradict the prisoners' statements.

Was this to be the final salvation of Abraham Braybrook and John Davis? No. Not entirely.

Plunkett declared that the burning of the bodies was:

> '... a criminal act being against common decency according to the notions of British civilisation ... and the two men should stand trial on that charge. This was in fact a mere misdemeanour.'

Plunkett believed that Allen should also be put on trial, but he left the final decision on that to Horatio Nelson Carrington, the Crown Prosecutor. Carrington declined to proceed against Allen, a remarkable decision, as it was he, by his own admission, who ordered the burning of the dead men. Captain Lonsdale quickly agreed to drop the murder charges and to proceed with only the misdemeanour.

The case of the Maiden Hill murders was the most controversial and talked about subject in the colony. All the way from the lowliest grog shanty to the membership of the embryonic Melbourne Club, it was the chief topic of conversation. Fame had found Abraham Braybrook and John Davis. Fame, but alas, definitely not fortune!

The trial, described on its conclusion by the *Gazette* as 'unparalleled in the criminal annals of the colony', was set down for August 8th in a court of Quarter Sessions before a Court Chairman and jury. The Crown Prosecutor was Horatio Nelson Carrington.

The police office, which served as a courtroom, was packed as the trial began. A jury of twelve was empanelled. They elected as foreman none other than leading citizen, publican, newspaper proprietor and co-founder of Melbourne, John Pascoe Fawkner. The balance of jurymen included Mister G. Lilly, whose drapery shop adjoined the Lamb Inn, a fine hotel popular with visiting squatters, Mr Marshall, a government immigration officer and Misters Harper, Hill, Gardiner, Landels, Lilly, Bingham, Jennings, Chisholm and Hood, all members of the more elite sections of society. All males of course. No women were permitted to serve on juries in those times.

Prosecutor Harrington had decided that the two men should face two counts – burning the bodies of the Dja dja wurrung men with a view to defeating the ends of justice; and indecently burning the bodies 'contrary to civilised usage'.

> James Davis and Abraham Brackbrook were indicted for a misdemeanor, in burning the bodies of two sable Aborigines. This trial being one that had caused a great excitement, the Crown Prosecutor had rejected in this case several jurors; the followng gentlemen were empanneled :— J. P. Fawkner, Foreman; and Messrs. Hill, Gardiner, Harper, Lilly, Dare, Landels, Lingham, Marshal, Jennings, Chisholm and Hood.
> These men had been first taken up for killing the persons whose bodies they afterwards burnt; but the Grand Jury of Sydney declined prosecuting them on that charge.

From The Port Phillip Patriot and Melbourne Advertiser, *12 August, 1839. Via Trove*

The court chairman, Irish barrister Edward Brewster, asked the men how they pleaded, and they both promptly replied 'guilty'.

What! Hang on a minute! That's not in the script! There was considerable surprise, and a wondering murmur went through the court. Crown Prosecutor Carrington rose and strongly advised the men to change their plea to 'not guilty'. Chairman Brewster, although more than a little puzzled, allowed the change. Phew! That was close.

Overseer Allen had been called as a witness for the prosecution, but curiously was not charged himself. He confirmed that Abraham Braybrook (misspelled as Brackbrook and Braidbrook etc. in several documents) and John Davis had burnt the bodies. In their defence, the men stated that they had been ordered to do so by their master, William Allen. The circumstances surrounding the shootings appeared to be irrelevant as Brewster ruled that they were assembled only to judge if the burning of the bodies was done illegally.

The judge, Brewster, summed up the proceedings with an instruction that if the jury was of the opinion that the two had not burned the bodies 'to frustrate the ends of justice', they must vote for an acquittal.

The jury left the room for a discussion in the street outside the court and returned in a few minutes with a 'not guilty' verdict, apparently not influenced by foreman John Pascoe Fawkner, whose editorials prior to the event indicated that he would favour a conviction. Perhaps his loyalties were divided. He was an ex-prisoner of the Crown himself, but was, according to his newspaper editorials, a supporter of Aborigines and the Protectorate. The court erupted in loud applause. (Later, Fawkner became a strong opponent of the protectorate system and went against Aborigines.)

Alas, it appeared however that Abraham and his companion would not be released from the hands of the law. Crown Prosecutor Carrington stepped in and ordered that Abraham and Davis not be returned to the Maiden Hills station but be placed under his own control and given over to work on roads and buildings in Melbourne. He further ordered that all of the twenty-three convicts originally assigned to Bowerman, now illegally held by the Learmonths at Maiden Hills, be similarly returned to Melbourne. This order was totally unexpected.

John Pascoe Fawkner, the Editor of the *Port Phillip Patriot*, wrote at length in support of the order.

> 'We fully and unequivocally agree with this determination on two grounds. One is the want of proper management evinced at the station; and the other is that nearly all troubles with the whites and Aborigines are between these white slaves and the black natives. These prisoners are subject to every indignity from their masters and they in turn tyrannize over, and frequently murder, the poor unenlightened Blacks. Slaves are invariably cowards and almost always cruel tyrants, if the opportunity offers.'

Harsh words indeed. Did this description apply to himself, editor John Pascoe Fawkner? Had he forgotten that he was a former prisoner of the crown? Had he hoped that nobody would know or recall his past? The item also called on Governor Gipps to withdraw all crown servants from the colony. Fat chance.

Robinson and Sievwright were most annoyed by the legal

manoeuvring of Crown Prosecutor Carrington and were bitterly disappointed in the verdict.

Abraham and his mate awaited their fate as workers on the chain gangs, probably unable to believe their luck.

There is little doubt that they shot and killed two Aborigines, but according to their statements, it seems it was self defence. Consider that they had a previously good relationship with the natives (perhaps too good!), so it seems very likely that there was some provocation. Plus, the men had a fear of overseer Allen who had ordered them to have no association with the bBacks and to chase them away at every opportunity.

Chapter Fifteen

Learmonth brothers. Bowerman dies. Loss of the Brittania. *Robinson visits Maiden Hills. Surprise meeting with Abraham. The Learmonths castigated by government. The Plenty River.*

In May of 1839, Henry Boucher Bowerman, continuing his expansive purchases of land, acquired a 640 acre lot subdivision on the Plenty River just outside Melbourne, in what is now the Heidelberg-Whittlesea district. It was potentially excellent and productive ground, but in many areas required clearing of the thick timber.

There was an increasing demand for firewood for home and industry and timber for construction work in the growing township of Melbourne. Contract woodcutters moved in, and the arduous work of clearing the land began. Bowerman's Plenty River purchase was made from the plan in Sydney, but in October of that year he had more important business to attend to that required his presence at Maiden Hills station.

He had decided to sell that lease, and two young and ambitious Scottish brothers, Thomas and Somerville Learmonth, had indicated a strong interest. The two men already held an extensive lease at Buninyong and had recently acquired a large area at nearby Trawalla (now the heritage listed property Ercildoune). The Learmonth brothers sealed a deal with Bowerman and added the Maiden Hills station to their impressive portfolio.

Bowerman undoubtedly made a large profit on the deal, which involved only the sale of his stock and improvements. Obviously the leased land could not be sold, but it was nevertheless valuable and the lease readily transferable. (Later, many such leaseholds could be purchased from the crown by selected occupants, such as the Learmonth brothers, for tiny sums.)

The sale completed, Bowerman prepared to make his way homeward, having promised his family that he would be home for Christmas. On November 11th, 1839 he boarded

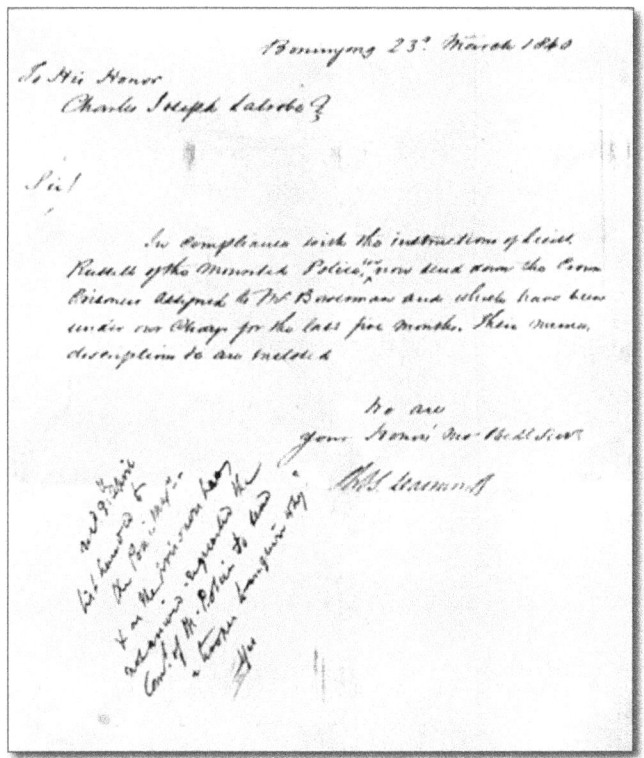

Letter from the Learmonth brothers to Governor Latrobe dated 1840 regarding the return of convicts to public service.

the coastal merchant ship *Brittania*, one of a half dozen passengers taken aboard for the journey to Sydney. They sailed on the morning of that day, and Henry Bowerman, his fellow passengers and the crew of the ship were never seen again. No trace was found, in spite of extensive searches for survivors organised after two weeks had elapsed, and it became obvious that the ship had foundered.

Months later, a longboat belonging to the *Brittania* was found on shore near Cape Howe. The boat had been pulled high onto the beach and was completely empty. It was believed that the boat had been beached by crew and passengers and that they had been attacked and killed by local natives. A search revealed no indication of the presence of the men and no trace of clothing, possessions or even human remains. The fate of Henry Boucher Bowerman will never be known.

* * *

The Plenty River above Whittlesea (Visit Melbourne).

Chief Protector of Aborigines George Robinson was not one to sit in his office in Melbourne. He was a 'hands on' man, and in February, 1840, he embarked on a tour of the districts. As he had done previously in Tasmania, he took his job seriously and wanted to see firsthand the people and territory for which he was responsible. He was accompanied by Assistant Protector Edward Stone Parker from the Franklinford protectorate.

On February 27th, 1840, they arrived near what was by this time Learmonth's property at Maiden Hills. Robinson kept a personal journal in which he wrote:

> 'Fine weather. Proceeded on foot to Learmonth's station over most rich and luxuriant grass. At four miles from camp and twelve miles from Pettitt's came to Learmonth's. I walked on alone leaving Mr P. to follow in the cart'.

It was at this point that Robinson received a shock. He wrote:

> 'The hut was in charge of Abraham Bingbuk [sic] one of the men who was charged with shooting blacks; Allen's case.'

He was astounded, and of course was referring to Abraham Braybrook and to William Allen. John Davis was also present. Robinson was obviously disturbed at the presence of men he still regarded as guilty of a serious crime against the people he was employed to protect.

He continued:

> 'I would remark here the injustice of the Government. These two men, it was clear on the trial, were not wholly cleared of guilt and which was the opinion of the Public Prosecutor who said that both the men, convicts, to be turned into the public works. And he said he would order all the men in. There was a large establishment of convicts. Yet here I find, when I visited the station, the very men returned who were tried, and of course the other[s] also'.

In the interim, Abraham and most of the convicts had been relocated by their new owners, the Learmonth brothers, to a spot between Mount Mitchell and Maiden Hills. The place is known still as Stud Road, as it was a stock breeding area. He had been placed in charge of a large group of convict workers, a reflection of Allen's confidence and trust.

Robinson was astonished to have discovered that the entire number of convicts/servants previously owned by Bowerman had somehow remained with the Learmonth's. This was contrary to the order made against Abraham and John Davis by the prosecutor (and his strong recommendation concerning the other twenty-one men) that they all be assigned to public works in Melbourne. Robinson then set

Old Mary [Noolermurneen] c1866, who cooked Murnong for Robinson in 1840.

off to Mount Cole to inspect that area, returning the next day to what he described as 'Abraham's'.

It would appear from this that Robinson struck some sort of rapport with Abraham. He and Parker camped the night with Abraham and the others and even shared an evening meal, including murnong prepared by native women and consumed around the campfire. The presence of the women indicates that Abraham, as the man in charge, must have somehow mended bridges with the natives.

There is nothing I have found to explain how Abraham

and Davis were returned to Maiden Hills in spite of Carrington's direct order and their assignment to himself! It is not certain if George Robinson lodged a complaint when he eventually returned to Melbourne, but it appears likely, as shortly thereafter, the Learmonth brothers received a written order to return all of their assigned servants to Melbourne. They promptly complied, albeit reluctantly, as they could not conduct their property without them, leading, shortly afterwards, to the sale of the northern part of their new run to Mr Robertson.

There was no penalty imposed on the brothers for what was in fact a breach of the law, as non-approved transfer of 'servants' was not permitted. The Learmonths were, of course, esteemed members of the squattocracy, the pure merinos.

There is no available evidence of precisely how Abraham came to be relocated to River Plenty and not put to work on 'public works', as ordered by the court. Following the sale of Maiden Hills station, we speculate that Abraham was chosen by Allen to accompany him to his new position as overseer at Bowerman's newly acquired property on the River Plenty. He had probably established considerable trust and even friendship for Abraham by that time. Whatever the reason, by the time the Learmonths received their orders to return the servants, Abraham was at the River Plenty. He had again escaped being transferred to the chain gangs.

Even though it was not far from Melbourne, the River

Plenty district was very isolated. Surveyed by Hoddle in 1838, it was reached only by a bush trail known as Ryrie's Track which wound its way through thick scrub and forest.

As a matter of interest, Batman's 'treaty' with the local Aborigines had been 'signed' by Jagga Jagga and Cooloolock on the banks of the Plenty, three kilometres above its junction with the Yarra. Their camp was at a lagoon on the Diamond Creek. The name, Nilumbick is all that survives of the tribe; all other traces have vanished. A sad case of 'Sorry'.

Similarly, I have found no evidence whatsoever to indicate how Abraham and Davis escaped assignment to the public works, and were returned to Maiden Hills station in violation of the order by the court. The most likely answer lies in the adage: 'It's not what you know, it's who you know'. The Learmonth brothers and Henry Boucher Bowerman were highly respected members of the Establishment and the newish Melbourne Club. What are friends for? Free labour was more than helpful to a squatter's profits.

Chapter Sixteen

*A Ticket of Leave. A Conditional Pardon. A marriage.
The River Plenty. Black Thursday.*

THIS story is well researched and factual. Limited licence for the sake of continuity and cohesion has been used by the writer, but the basic content has been thoroughly researched and it is believed accurate.

A great deal of detail about Abraham's life at River Plenty cannot be found. However, it appears logical that he may have worked, at least initially, for William Allen on the Bowerman property there. This was conducted on behalf of Bowerman's estate until some years later. Henry Bowerman Junior mortgaged the property to Mort and Co. for eight hundred pounds in 1842, and after seven years of non-repayment they seized it in 1849. In much later years the property was taken up by the government as a water catchment for the Yan Yean reservoir and has been closed ever since.

It is also possible that he worked for Thomas Wills who was a holder of large lease areas there at this time. However, the most likely scenario is that he was the recipient of a government grant of ten acres which came into effect for deserving Ticket of Leave men at around that time. No record of this grant has yet been found, but how else could he have become a farmer?

How Abraham came to meet and marry Eliza Francis of

Collingwood is also a matter for speculation. At the time of their marriage on July 7th, 1842, River Plenty was a considerable distance from Collingwood, but it was passed through on the way between the Plenty River and Melbourne Town. Maybe they met in passing?

It is far more likely that Eliza was employed as a domestic servant on one of the number of rich properties such as Horden's or Thomas Wills's Estate and they met there, but there is no available evidence of this.

What we do know is that the Government of New South Wales did not readily approve of marriage of current convicts to free women such as Eliza. Such marriages were described as 'not wise' and were discouraged by the authorities. Only if a man was already assigned to a single or widowed woman who owned property was it acceptable. However, Eliza was obviously not a property owner, so how the marriage was approved is a mystery. If a free woman took the unusual step of marrying a man such as Abraham, who was still a convict, or did not hold a Ticket of Leave, the rules said that she must share, at least to some extent, her husband's status. Eliza was certainly not a convict and had no criminal record.

Why Eliza took the step of marriage to a convict we will never know; any number of free men were available. We assume that in Eliza's case it was deep affection. Convict men often saw marriage as a way to leading a sober, steady and reformed life.

Eliza was the daughter of Thomas and Celia Francis, free immigrants from County Wexford, Ireland; presumably forced out by the first potato famine and English oppression. They came to the colony at Melbourne in 1840 on the *Calcutta*. Eliza is described in shipping records as aged twenty and an illiterate protestant. The family included a son Thomas, and another daughter Celia. Nothing is known of the Francis family's Irish past as all records from the Exford county were apparently destroyed in a fire many years ago.

As he was still a convict, Abraham had first to obtain the consent of the governor to marry. He would have had to fill out the 'Convicts Application to Marry' form to lodge with the authorities and gain approval. No doubt he had much assistance with this, as he had never learnt to read and write. The marriage was conducted by Reverend A.C. Thompson in July 1842 and was held in the original rough timber building, the Pioneers Church which was built in 1837. The present stone building was under construction on the site and not yet in service. It was located on Batman's land at the corner of William Street and Little Collins Street and was shared by Anglicans and Presbyterians, until the latter were forced out by the Anglicans in controversial circumstances. (The Anglican Church has never been noted for its Christian attitudes where property and wealth are concerned!)

In 1913–1914, the 'new' building was moved, stone by stone, to its present site in King Street opposite the Flagstaff Gardens. By then the value of the land on which it rested was immense and the lure of so much cash irresistible. St James Old Cathedral remains one of Melbourne's most treasured historical landmarks.

Good news! On March 11th, 1843, Abraham was awarded a Ticket of Leave (ref. 43/606 Authority #28). This enabled him to move about more or less freely and it was a welcome event, a step closer to a pardon.

We already know that Abraham was a shoemaker, and he described himself as such on October 18th, 1843 on the baptism certificate of his first son William (following the common practice of naming children after the father's parents). A daughter Anne came within a year.

Three years later, on June 27th, 1847, Abraham was described as a farmer on the baptism certificate of his second son, Isaac (the author's grandfather). Another year, and daughter Elizabeth (Eliza) was born. Abraham Junior* followed in 1850. All the baptisms took place at what was by then the new St James Cathedral.

On December 12th, 1848, Governor FitzRoy signed Abraham's Conditional Pardon. It became official on February 1st, 1849 when entered into the official records in Sydney (ref. p249/250 Reg. # 33). Sydney of course remained the headquarters for the Port Phillip District until separation a little over a year later. A conditional pardon allowed

---

* *Abraham junior became a publican at Woodford, seven kilometres on the Mortlake road from Warrnambool. He married Annie Gray at Ballarat c.1878 and had one son William (b. 1879 at Woodford) from whom it is probable that the Warrnambool branch of the family descended. Abraham junior died aged only thirty-three in January, 1883. It seems likely that he had worked for a time in the mines at Ballarat, as he died from phthisis, a lung disease common among miners.*

Woodford, near Warrnambool. Abraham Jr. had a hotel here.

Abraham complete freedom, but specifically forbade his ever returning to Great Britain.

Along the way, Abraham was able to acquire his small parcel of land and become a farmer. Of the twenty-one small farmers registered in the area at that time, although all were unnamed, one was described in official documents as being a 'shoemaker'. The odds are that this person was Abraham.

We can only imagine what life was like for Eliza and her little family at River Plenty. They no doubt lived in a slab hut with a bark roof, typical of the area, perhaps two tiny rooms with dirt floors and a detached kitchen. Whatever it was, we can be certain that it was a rough camp with few conveniences and no luxuries. A hard life, but it was not unusual for the poor class of the time. Undoubtedly Eliza worked hard and made the home as attractive and comfortable as she could. There is no indication as to the precise locality of the home, although it would have been adjacent to a water supply, most likely very near the Plenty River.

It is most unlikely that Abraham and Eliza's children were able to attend a school in this lightly populated and isolated district, although large properties sometimes made arrangement for limited education for staff families. The district was a centre for timber getting for the growing township of Melbourne, and many of the men were engaged in that industry. Perhaps Abraham turned his hand to that to earn cash.

A most notable event in the second half of the 19th century was the disastrous and tragic fires of Black Thursday. At Plenty River it began on the Scrubby Mountain station and roared in from the north, driven by a raging wind. It destroyed twelve square miles of property along the Plenty River alone, taking homes, crops and fences galore. Over one hundred people were left homeless, representing a majority of the district's population. Burnt homes, sheds, fences, trees and dead and dying stock littered the dreadful scene. It is hard to comprehend, an estimated one half of the state was devastated by the series of massive fires on that day. Numerous people died terrible deaths. The actual numbers will never be known, so widespread were the fires, but certainly well over one hundred died.

In March of 1851, the following notice appeared in the Melbourne newspapers.

> To the charitable public of Victoria.
>
> 'Messrs. Bennett and Duff beg to lay before the public the list of subscriptions collected by them towards the relief of the sufferers by the late conflagration in the Plenty District. We beg to call the attention to the feeling public to the very trying, helpless state to which a few respectable and industrious farmers on the Plenty have been reduced by the late fire. Those in which this is in aid of those who have lost all their property.
>
> 'The names of those to whom this subscription is being raised are Patrick Kenny, James Patten, – Maxwell, – Watson, A Braybrook, John Hunter, – McLeod and another.
>
> 'The total loss to all the people of the Plenty was said to exceed six thousand pounds. It was expected that the money raised would amount to less than half of that sum.'*

From this we know that Abraham and Eliza were one of eight families that had lost everything they possessed. We

---

* *According to the Argus of 11 April, 1851, the subscription raised a promised 295 pounds 11s and 6d (of which 239 pounds 4s 6d had been received).*

Melbourne 1854 by Robert Russell.

can only imagine the horror experienced by them and their five children, William, Isaac, Annie, Elizabeth and six month old Abraham.

However, a graphic account of this fire and its ferocity is given in John Chandler's *Forty years in the Wilderness*, edited by noted Historian, Michael Cannon.

Chandler was inside the holocaust. He and his father had gone to the area to harvest timber for fencing. Following are extracts from his account:

> We saw that the ranges were all on fire. It was burning on both sides of the track. It was not safe so we went back to the river. It was fearfully appalling to be surrounded by the whole country on fire. It got into the crops and the wheat fields seem to light up all over at once, like a huge furnace. It was a most terrible sight. I can never forget it. The roar of the fires as they met was appalling. We had to put our mouths in the dust to get our breath. The trees were burning right to their tops. I could not see one yard in front of me.

> The noise of the fires and the falling timber was enough to try the nerves of a stronger man than me. – I made for the river. The splitters had to stand in water up to their knees to save their lives.
>
> (The morning after.)
>
> All was a black mass of smouldering timber. They had everything burnt, leaving wife and children without cover or clothing. Oh it was pitiful. The scene was one of desolation for miles. There were a great number of farmers burnt all along the Plenty River as far as Greensborough, more than twenty miles we travelled, all burnt.

This was a ghastly, devastating fire, the fiercest in modern Australian history; many, many died. Along with a dozen others, the fire destroyed Abraham and Eliza's home, all of its contents, their crops and their animals. We have no idea how the family survived, and how can we imagine the horror and loss they endured? They were left with nothing but the clothes they wore. My God! How could a person front up to life under those hopeless circumstances?

But continue they did, we know not how. The money and goods from public subscription, plus the community goodwill, would have been a great comfort.

Too soon came a tragic completion of the family disaster. On July 14th, 1851, five months after the fire and still recovering from the shocking ordeal, Abraham died. It is fair to assume that the fire and its awful effects were a strong contributor to his early death, age forty.

There is no record of his death, other than that of the funeral celebrant, held in the records of St Mark's Anglican Church in Melbourne. There is nothing to indicate the cause of his early death, nor even irrefutable evidence of where he is buried. The careful research undertaken by Alan Braybrook, Glenn Braybrook and the writer indicates that he almost certainly lies beneath the Queen Victoria Market, the site of Melbourne's first cemetery, where some 10 000 were interred. Only about 1 000 were disinterred for removal to the new cemetery when the site became a market, although there was some pretence that all were removed.

It appears likely that only those with headstones were moved, and Abraham undoubtedly occupied an unmarked

Eliza , wife of Abraham, pictured when she was in her mid-seventies and had become Eliza Black.

pauper's grave. The land occupied by the pioneer dead of Port Phillip was far too close to the developing city and too valuable to remain a cemetery! It was, they said, the perfect site for a large market.

On July 17th, Abraham's body was conveyed by dray, probably from what passed for his home, most likely direct to the cemetery for the graveside service conducted by the Reverend Clowes in a busy day for the Vicar at St Mark's, as he had at least two funerals listed.

How tragic must the death of Abraham been for Eliza. With no income and no man to help, it would have been a terrible ordeal for her. There were no pensions, and the only relief available came from the churches, or sometimes from equally poor neighbours or, rarely, the better off.

I weep for my great-grandmother Eliza Braybrook, an Australian hero.

Chapter Seventeen

Eliza moves on. Robert Black. A marriage.
Ballarat. Belfast or Belfast?

SOON after the death of her husband, Eliza and family somehow found their way to Indented Head. As one would expect, Eliza sought family for help and support. Fortunately she had such family. Her brother Thomas had settled at Indented Head, married to Esther Black, daughter of James and Margaret, who had migrated from County Derry, Ireland, arriving in Melbourne in February, 1842. Also living with the family was Esther's brother, Robert Black. Like so many men in this colony, Robert Black was on the lookout for a wife. At that time the entire Bellarine Peninsula was known as Indented Head, so it is difficult to pinpoint with any accuracy where the Black family lived.

Another tragedy struck Eliza when her two-year-old daughter Elizabeth died. Her burial place is unknown, but possibly it is Geelong. We do not know the circumstances of her death.

At that time, a woman with children, left destitute on the death of a husband, had few choices; she could find some sort of job, but with young children to care for, where? She could perhaps find work as a housemaid – very difficult with children – she could become a prostitute, as was common, or she could find a husband.

In Eliza's favour was her relatively young age and a scarcity of women in a land where men far outnumbered women. One would have to say that she was fortunate enough to find a man who apparently cared well for her and her brood. Robert Black and Eliza married in the Church of Scotland, Geelong on May 31st, 1852 and shortly after moved away to seek gold in the rush to Magpie, Ballarat, where they remained until death.

* * *

Interestingly, Eliza and Abraham's sons, Isaac and William, married two Bowerman sisters; Isaac married Emily and William married Elizabeth. The girls' parents were John and Elizabeth Bowerman, originally from Tasmania. John was a baker, and at the time of the marriages they appear to have had a bakery in Ballarat. The name Bowerman is no more than a coincidence, with no relationship to Henry Boucher Bowerman, Abraham's one-time master.

We know that Elizabeth Bowerman was born in Tasmania and Emily at Belfast. It is possible that the family moved from Tasmania by ship to Belfast (Port Fairy), but it is also possible that it refers to the Belfast near Amphitheatre in the Avoca-Lexton district. No evidence either way has been found. John may have had a bakery at one time at this Belfast, however, it is far more likely to have been at Belfast/Port Fairy, a thriving settlement, before relocating to Ballarat.

The Amphitheatre district Belfast's existence was unknown to me until the late 1990s. It is identified only by a small roadside sign that proclaims Belfast Cemetery. No sign of a settlement exists. Nor of a cemetery! Speaking to a local farmer who lived for years near the cemetery road, he stated that he had never heard of the cemetery!

As a matter of interest, Eliza and Robert Black went on to have five children together, Wesley, 1853, Emily, 1855 (who died when only eight), Margaret, 1856 (who died within hours of birth), another Margaret, 1857 and James 1860.

Fortunately (thereby preventing much confusion for later generations seeking their ancestors), Eliza's children by Abraham remained Braybrook and did not take the name of their stepfather, Robert Black. The Braybrooks and the Blacks have stayed on in Ballarat until the present day.

They didn't find a lot of gold!

The End

Appendix

In 1834, the Braybrook family were apparently well established in Essex, but the origin of the name is obscure. It is possible that the family was at some time employed by the Barons of Braybrook or even the Norman gentry, the Gerrard and Lady Anne De Braybrook family. Peasants often took the name of their masters as a means of identity.

A Lord Braybrooke was created in 1788, some relative of the Howard family who owned the magnificent Audley End mansion at Saffron Walden, built in the seventeenth century. King Charles II once owned it and set up his court there. Saffron Walden was named after the saffron plant, used for dyes, condiments and medicines, which was an important industry in the area until the late eighteenth century. It is extremely unlikely that the aristocratic Lord Braybrooke had any connection to the very humble Braybrook family of Kelvedon.

From early records, it seems that the Braybrook family had its roots in Essex, within close proximity of Kelvedon. A Braybrook is mentioned in the Quarter Sessions of Chelmsford as early as 1616.

Interestingly, in this current era, there is no-one that recalls any Braybrook living in the Kelvedon area, which is peculiar, as they were present, although not necessarily numerous, in the eighteenth and nineteenth centuries.

The last Braybrook mentioned in Kelvedon district records is Arthur Braybrook, age fifteen, son of Ann, noted in the census of 1861. The first certain mention of the family is in the records of the St Mary the Virgin Church at Kelvedon, 19th August, 1757 when Thomas married Sarah Jones. Mr S. Sumner performed the ceremony. Neither of the pair could write and they marked their names in the customary manner, in Thomas' case a peculiar looking half circle.

The couple had seven children – Sarah, William, John, John (the first John died age two), Joelene, Isaac and finally, in 1777, an Abraham. Although no record can be found, it is likely that William was to become the father of our Abraham. He married Anne and they registered three children

St Mary The Virgin Church, Kelvedon. Thomas Braybrook and Sarah Thomas were married here in 1757 and buried here in 1808.

William (1802), Rachel (1808) and Abraham (1811). This ties in pretty well with Abraham's age when convicted and sentenced in 1834.

We do not know what became of all the children of Thomas and Sarah Braybrook, grand-parents of our Abraham. Thomas died on November 6th, 1808, aged seventy-five and Sarah nine days later. Both are buried at St Andrews church. We do know that Sarah Junior married James Clements at Kelvedon in November 1781 and the Clement name is still well known in the area. Isaac died on January 29th, 1855, aged eighty-one, Abraham on January 9th, three years later. Both are buried in the churchyard at St Mary's.

This story has an odd ending. Rachel*, the sister of Abraham, made her way to Australia in 1866, many years after she married John Storey in 1835. John had come to the colony with their son James in 1855, probably to seek his fortune. All the easier won gold had petered out by the time the two arrived at Ballarat, and John won no fortune. Eventually, he was able to bring his wife here, but sadly, she was already suffering from breast cancer. They settled at Kangaroo Flat, Staffordshire Reef south of Ballarat where Rachel soon died. She is buried in the Staffordshire Reef Cemetery.

As mentioned, when Abraham Braybrook died, his widow Eliza married Robert Black at Geelong (1852). Their daughter, Margaret, married George McKay. Coincidentally,

---

* *Some say that Rachel was a cousin and not the daughter of William, but we are unconvinced.*

George and Margaret's daughter Una, married a Milton Storey in 1938. It is believed that he was a descendent of John and Ann Storey, the same John Storey who married Rachel, mentioned above.

Australian pioneer Abraham, was born in 1811, probably at Kelvedon. His mother was Ann (Mary according to newspaper accounts of Abraham's trial). We do not know of his siblings, except Rachel, but in those days it is likely there were several. An Isaac is known of and there is an Anne mentioned in church records who could have been a sister. She is mentioned as having a bastard daughter Emma Frances, early in 1845 and again, a bastard son Arthur, late in 1845. (They told it as it was back then!) In Arthur's case his father is named as Thomas, but this has later been crossed out. Bastards are not new to the Braybrook family it seems!

The historic church of St Mary the Virgin stands alongside the ancient highway built by the Romans in the twelfth century which runs from Colchester to London. Parts of the church from the twelfth century are still standing, incorporating quoins of Roman brick. It was added to in the thirteenth century.

There is certain proof of the church's early existence in the records that describe the appointment of the Vicar of Kelvedon in 1356.

Acknowledgements

The Chronicles of early Melbourne.
University of Melbourne Library.
State Library of Victoria.
State Library of NSW.
Public Records Office, London.
Curator St James Old Cathedral.
Curator St Marks Anglican Church.
Archives Authority of NSW.
Victorian Public Records Office.
The records of the church of St Mary the Virgin, Kelvedon.
Maritime Archives, London.
Alan Braybrook, Broken Hill, NSW.
Frank Braybrook, Runaway Bay, Qld.
Glenn Braybrook, Forest Creek, Chewton, Victoria.
Castlemaine Library and Staff.
Margaret Roberts, Scarsdale Victoria.
Bruce and Margaret Zusner.
Thanks to John Tully of Dunolly, Victoria for his assistance and allowing reproduction of his valuable photographs.
Special thanks to Bernard Schultz of Level Heading for his dedicated work in lay-up, editing suggestions and sage advice.

Special thanks to my publisher and life partner, Marilyn Bennet.

Bibliography and References

Michael Cannon 1991, *Old Melbourne Town,* Loch Haven Books.

Michael Cannon, *Historical Records of Victoria Vols. 1, 3, 2b, 7,* Vic. Govt. Printing Office.

Margaret Oulton, *A Valley of the Finest Description,* Shire of Lexton.

Rita Hull 1992, *Henry Boucher Bowerman, an ambitious pioneer.*

David John Wilkinson 1969, *Diamond Valley 1836-1854* Thesis (MA). Ref. 23142873.

The Port Phillip Patriot.

The Port Phillip Gazette.

Michael Cannon 1982, *Who's master? Who's man?* Currey O'Neil, Melbourne.

Stan Jarvis 1979, *A View into Essex,* Terence Dalton Ltd.

Charles Bateson 1969, *The Convict Ships,* Brown, Son and Ferguson.

J. Randell *1980, Yaldwyn of the Golden Spurs, Mast Gully Press, Melbourne.*

Journal of George Augustus Robinson – Vol.1.

Edward Curr 1883, *Recollections of Squatting in Victoria.* Melbourne University Press.

Index of Names and Places

A

Allen, William – 55–61, 63–65, 66–73, 74, 77, 81–90, 91, 94, 96, 98, 103–111, 111–117, 122–127, 131–134, 136
Arthur, Sir George (Gov.) – 43
Aston Station – 55, 56
Atkinson, James – 55
Atlas, HMS – 34
Australia Felix – 61, 71

B

Batman, John – 86, 135, 138
Bayley, George – 37
Black
    Esther – 147
    James and Margaret – 147
Black Thursday – 141
Blackwater River – 15
Bombala – 56
Boucher, Marion – 51
Bourke, Sir Richard (Gov.) – 43, 85, 100
Bowerman
    Emily and William – 148
    John and Elizabeth – 148
Bowerman, Henry Boucher – 49–61, 63, 70, 82–85, 94, 103, 106, 126, 128–135, 148, 157
    Henry Bowerman, Jr – 136
Bowman, William – 80
Braybrook
    Abraham, Jr. – 139
    Ann – 21
    Anne – 139
    Elizabeth – 139
    Isaac – 139, 143, 148, 152, 153, 154
    William – 139
Brennan, Denis – 33, 71, 83, 87, 87–91, 96, 107, 108, 115
Brewster, Edward – 124, 125
Britannia, HMS – 32
Brittania, HMS – 130
Brown, John Sylvester ('Paddy') – 63, 74
Budge, Henry – 53, 56
Buninyong – 105, 117, 128

C

Calcutta, HMS – 138
Campaspe River – 80
Carlsruhe – 76
Carrington, Horatio Nelson – 123–127, 134
Castlemaine – 79
Chelmsford – 20
Coffe, William – 53, 59
Collector – 54
Constable Sparrow – 20, 21
Cooma – 56
Coppock, John – 63, 75, 76, 80, 89

D

Dagnar, Henry – 120
Davis, John – 53–59, 71, 83, 87, 91, 114, 116, 118, 121–125, 131, 132
Dennot, Thomas – 33, 34
Devine, John – 59
Devine, Johnny – 53, 59
Doctors Creek – 85, 87, 89, 93. See also Mammaloid Creek

E
Ebden, Charles – *80*
Emson, James – *16, 18*
Ermington – *49, 50*
Expedition Pass – *78*

F
Fawkner, John Pascoe – *86, 123, 125, 126*
Female Factory – *40*
Field of Mars – *49*
FitzRoy, Sir Charles Augustus (Gov.) – *139*
Fleming, John – *119, 120*. See also Myall Creek Massacre
Flinders Island – *102*
Flinter's Forge – *69*
Forest Creek – *78*
Francis
  Celia – *137, 138*
  Eliza – *136–145, 147–149, 153*
  Thomas – *137, 138, 147*
Franklinford – *104, 131*

G
Gipps, Major Sir George (Gov.) – *121, 126*
Goulburn River – *75*
Grenada, HMS – *51*
Gundagai – *69*
Gunning – *54*

H
Hellen, Timothy – *17, 18, 20, 21, 22, 25*
Higgins, Henry – *53*
Higgins, Patrick – *59*
Hillsborough, HMS – *34, 35*
Hooghly, HMS – *34, 35, 36, 37, 44, 46*
Howlong – *72*

I
Indented Head – *147*
Indigo Creek – *73*
Inworth – *15*

J
Jenkins, John – *53, 59*
Jugiong Creek – *69*
Julien Range (Jullian) – *105, 106*

K
Kelvedon – *15, 20, 44, 151, 152, 153, 154, 155*
Kyneton – *80*

L
Lady Nugent, HMS – *91*
Langstone Harbour – *27*
Latrobe, Charles Joseph (Gov.) – *87, 118, 129*
Learmonth, Thomas and Somerville – *106, 126, 128–134*
Lerida – *54, 56, 60*
Leviathan, HMS – *27, 46*
Lexton – *80*
Lhotsky, Johann – *56*
Loddon River – *79, 81*
Lonsdale, William – *84, 87, 98, 100, 103, 104, 107, 118, 122, 123*
Loveless, George – *44, 48*. See also Tolpuddle Martyrs

M
Maiden Hills – *82, 85, 98, 103–106, 116, 118, 125–134*
Maldon, England – *15, 26*
Malmsbury – *80*
Mammaloid Creek – *85, 87, 106*. See also Doctors Creek
Mammaloid Hills – *82*
Marion – *50, 52*

McDonald, Alexander – *49*
Metcalfe – *80*
Miller, E.B. – *49, 50*
Mitchell, Major Thomas – *61, 64, 106*
Mollison, Alexander – *80*
Monaro – *55, 56, 58*
Moreton Bay – *51*
Mount Cole – *133*
Mount Mitchell – *81, 132*
Mount Warrenheip – *105, 106*
Mullengandra – *71*
Murnong – *95, 133*
Murrumbidgee River – *69*
Myall Creek – *119, 120*

N
Newstead – *79*

O
Oliver, James – *71*
Ovens River – *74*

P
Parker, Edward Stone – *104, 131*
Parkinson, William – *16, 18, 21*
Phillip, Admiral Arthur (Gov.) – *49*
Plenty River – *128, 130, 141, 144*
Plunkett, John – *122, 123*
Port Macquarie – *51*
Port Phillip – *62, 63, 76, 85, 87, 101, 102, 105, 118, 121, 124, 126, 139, 146, 157*
Portsmouth – *26–34, 34, 37, 46*
Pye
  Phillip – *21*
  Pye, Henry – *17, 19, 20, 21, 25*
Pyrenees Range – *81, 105*

Q
Queen Victoria Market – *145*

R
Reed, Joe – *21*
Robert Black – *147, 148, 149, 153*
Robinson, George Augustus – *101, 101–110, 118, 121, 126, 131–134, 157*
Rose Farm – *49, 50*
Royal Admiral, HMS – *34, 35*

S
Sievwright, Charles Wightman – *96, 102–119, 126*
Swampy River – *75*
Sydney Town – *37, 38, 50, 120*

T
Tank Stream – *38*
Taylor, James – *53*
Taylor, Samuel – *36*
The Knackers – *27*
Therry, Father John – *70*
The Ship, Inworth – *16, 21*
Thomas Mitchell – *61, 64, 81, 110*
Ticket of Leave – *136*
Tolpuddle Martyrs – *44, 48*

V
Vaux, James Hardy – *28*

W
Waterloo, HMS – *91*
Wells, William – *58*
Wills, Thomas – *136, 137*

Y
Yaldwyn, William – *63, 65, 67, 69, 70, 74, 75, 80, 89*
Yarra – *86, 100, 135*
Yass – *54, 56, 60, 63, 65*
Yass River – *69*

Other Titles by Ian Braybrook

The Changing Times
Ian Braybrook was a radio broadcaster for many years. His childhood and early teen years are far removed from the 'glamour' of that job. The unique adventures and misadventures crammed into his first 18 years of life provide a fascinating read. At the same time, this is an important record of the way life was for some in the depression and post-depression era.

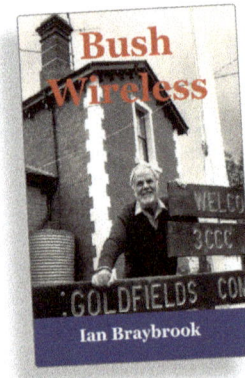

Bush Wireless
This is the wonderful story that spans the 37 years of Ian's life as a popular radio broadcaster. In it the reader will meet a myriad of interesting people and learn of the pioneering of fm radio in Central Victoria. Ian met and came to know hundreds of people from all walks of life.

Gweneth Wisewould – Outpost Doctor.
The story of a unique Australian – Gweneth Wisewould MBS – a society belle and brilliant surgeon who, at the age of 57 moved from Melbourne to the remote outpost of Trentham in Victoria's Central Highlands. The story of her life, her triumphs, her friends and personal tragedies makes fascinating reading.

Sarah's Search – A Silk Odyssey.

This is a must read account of the efforts of one woman to establish a silk industry in Harcourt and Corowa, Australia. It tells of the passionate resolve of widow, Sarah Florentia Bladen Neill, who had a vision for her country and the courage to fight for it. Hers was a mammoth effort and her story, never before told, deserves a prominent place in Australia's history. (Co-written with Marilyn Bennet.)

All titles are available from selected bookshops or direct from the publisher, ianandmazza@gmail.com or phone 0409 333 513.

www.ingramcontent.com/pod-product-compliance
Lightning Source LLC
Chambersburg PA
CBHW051547010526
44118CB00022B/2616